Meaningful Course Revision

MEANINGFUL COURSE REVISION
Enhancing Academic Engagement Using Student Learning Data

Catherine M. Wehlburg
TEXAS CHRISTIAN UNIVERSITY

Anker Publishing Company, Inc.
Bolton, Massachusetts

MEANINGFUL COURSE REVISION
Enhancing Academic Engagement
Using Student Learning Data

ISBN 1-933371-05-6

Composition by Tanya Anoush Johnson, Senior Designer
Cover design by Dutton & Sherman Design

Anker Publishing Company, Inc.
563 Main Street
P.O. Box 249
Bolton, MA 01740-0249 USA

www.ankerpub.com

Library of Congress Cataloging-in-Publication Data
Wehlburg, Catherine.
    Meaningful course revision : enhancing academic engagement using student learning data / Catherine M. Wehlburg.
        p. cm.
Includes bibliographical references (p.).
    ISBN 1-933371-05-6
    1. Educational evaluation. 2. Curriculum change. 3. Educational tests and measurements. 4. Lesson plans. 5. Active learning. I. Title.
    LB2822.75.W44 2006
    371.3'028—dc22

                                    2006004169

Table of Contents

About the Author

Catherine Wehlburg is currently the executive director of the Office for Assessment and Quality Enhancement at Texas Christian University. Prior to this, she worked as the director of the William H. Koehler Center for Teaching Excellence, also at Texas Christian University.

She earned a Ph.D. in educational psychology from the University of Florida in 1992 and took a faculty position at Stephens College in 1991 where she taught in the psychology department and began to explore the interplay between faculty development and assessment at the university level.

Dr. Wehlburg has edited or coedited four volumes of *To Improve the Academy* (Anker, 2001–2004) and has published several articles and book chapters on assessment and faculty development. In 1998 she worked as a senior associate at the American Association for Higher Education in the Assessment Forum while on sabbatical. In addition, she has been a consultant-evaluator for the Higher Learning Commission and for the Southern Association of Colleges and Schools.

Preface

After more than a decade as a faculty member and many years of working with faculty, I am convinced that many of the course changes that faculty make are based on reasons other than data, such as intuition or single student comments. While these may be important guides in determining when to make course revision decisions, alone they are not sufficient. Data is essential for many reasons: accreditation associations are mandating it; higher education constituents want to know what students are learning. Because of these external requirements, many institutions are regularly, albeit often grudgingly, accepting the fact that information on student learning needs to be collected. But we should be collecting this information anyway—and faculty have been doing this all along. We know which students have performed well on exams or projects, we know which students in our classes are the "good" students and which ones need additional work. We need multiple measures of meaningful student learning that we can use to discover what students are learning and can base our course decision-making upon.

Information about student learning is part of the teaching and learning relationship, and we should continue to collect it. Faculty measure student learning and can then assign grades, but much of the actual information about student learning (not grades, but direct measures of learning) can and should be used for other purposes. Reporting information about student learning to our institutions in the form of a program review or to make a regional or specialized accreditation team happy are not the primary purposes for knowing how much our students are learning. Instead, we must do it so that we know what is working in our teaching, what we can do to enhance student learning, and what should be added or changed in our courses to enhance the academic integration of our students.

Changing the activities and design of a course is a great deal of work, and focusing that work so that student learning is the reason for change is essential. Even though a single negative comment from a student's end-of-semester course evaluation may sting, changing a course just because of that comment minimizes the opportunity to look at multiple sources of data about what students are learning in your courses. By collecting and using information about how well students are reaching your course goals, you will be better able to know what impact your changes are having on student learning. Putting your course into a cycle of continual revision and constant improvement will benefit your students, and it will also keep your teaching interesting, fresh, and enjoyable.

Writing this book has been an enjoyable experience. Many people were involved in the process, and I would like to thank the department chairs and other faculty at Texas Christian University who read through chapters of this book, used information from them, and gave meaningful and significant feedback about what was helpful and what was not. A very special thank you to Billie Hara, who not only read many of the chapters but gave me constant encouragement and support during the writing process.

In addition to my colleagues, I would especially like to note the support and encouragement of my family. My husband George Krasowsky and my daughter Brooke were enthusiastic listeners to portions of the manuscript. Even though Brooke is five years old at the time of this writing, she became a very special writing partner. She began "writing" her books while I was working on mine. I have to admit that her use of color and graphics is much better than mine and many readers might wish for her hearts, flowers, and butterflies to be printed in the margins of the manuscript.

Catherine Wehlburg
Texas Christian University
October 2005

Chapter One

Data-Based Decision-Making

*E*ach semester it happens: courses are revised, different textbooks are ordered, and new syllabi are developed. But what really goes into the decision-making process of course revision or even new course development? In many cases, the decision-making is based on student responses to end-of-course evaluations or off-the-cuff student comments. Sometimes, the instructor of the course decides that enough has changed in the field to warrant changes in the course. These are all valid reasons for making changes, but what really should be changed? What should be kept? What worked to increase student learning and understanding? Without appropriate and meaningful data, these questions are very difficult to answer. Without answers, the changes in the course may not work to increase student learning. Even worse, a lot of effort and energy could be put into something that might actually decrease student learning.

The purpose of this book is to illustrate the appropriate use of student learning outcomes data to enhance course development and course revision. The concept of data-based course design is part of the paradigm shift from teacher-centered to student-centered learning. In student-centered learning, the focus is on the student—what the student is doing, demonstrating, and saying. But, just asking students how they like the class or what you should change in the course is not necessarily going to guide course revision toward increasing student learning. However, these types of "satisfaction" questions and their answers often do guide course revision. Faculty sometimes change their courses because students aren't happy with the amount of homework assignments or the way the class is conducted. While these are valid concerns (and certainly enough to prompt considering course revision), they don't tell us anything about how much a student is learning and whether there is any transfer of that learning within the course or within a sequence of courses. To obtain the type of information that will guide meaningful course revision, different types of questions need to be asked. In some cases these questions have already been incorporated into the course or departmental assessment process.

These questions are sometimes called learning outcomes or learning objectives. They can be used to gather information on what students are learning, and, more importantly, what students are not learning. Some of these measures look at department-level outcomes. For example, there may be a senior-level exam that all students take, or a portfolio assignment that is used to assess skills across the major. These departmental assessment measures are important and can also be used to look at individual courses.

In order to use departmental measures for a course, you first need to identify the learning outcomes that you are interested in. In other words, what skills or knowledge do you want students to demonstrate as a result of your class? Once you have that information you can look at the departmental measure and determine if there is a portion of that measurement instrument that indicates those student outcomes.

For example, in the psychology department of a small Midwestern college, graduating seniors are required to submit a psychology portfolio that includes an original student research report, a clinical observation analysis, and a paper that demonstrates APA-style writing. The instructor of a course called Research Methods was interested in seeing if students were learning appropriate research methodology. While there were in-class assignments that required this, it wasn't until the senior year that students were required to do original research. By looking at the senior portfolios and focusing on the research paper, the instructor was able to see where students were learning information and what they still were not demonstrating by the senior year. This information was used to overhaul the course so that students could demonstrate appropriate knowledge and use of research methods multiple times in the course. Over the next several years, the scores on the research methods portion of the psychology portfolio improved (and thus the students were learning more and were using the learning more appropriately). By using department-level data, the course instructor was able to redesign the course to better meet the learning needs of the students.

Department-level assessment can be helpful, but it is sometimes easier and more appropriate to look at course-level assessment measures to determine what students are learning. This type of data is directly applicable to what you want to know in order to revise a course. Some of this information can be gained from existing course assignments. For example, in a southern university, students in an education course are expected to be able to apply specific theories to classroom situations by using case study analysis and problem solving. Students submit these assignments throughout the semester and the instructor is able to tailor the assignment based on the previous assignment results. At the end of the semester, data concerning students' understanding and application skills with regard to educational theory was compiled. Based on these data, the instructor modified the assignments and the sequencing of the case studies so that students were exposed to a wider variety of classroom situations and theories. This increased the knowledge base of the students and improved final exam scores.

If your questions are not being asked at the department level, the answers to these questions can in many cases be found within a course. Students demonstrate how much they are learning in various ways throughout the semester in any given course. Exams, papers, and class discussions are only some of the methods faculty use to collect data on student learning. Often faculty go through a typical process to assign end-of-semester grades: create assignments, present information to students, collect student work, and assign grades based on the student work. The final grade is not what we are interested in when it comes to course revision, however. The work that a student submits (even before it is graded) is the data that can inform course revision. A faculty member who asks student learning questions at this point can often find out what students know, and more importantly, what they do not seem to know. Identifying when and why to ask student learning questions is important.

Using existing sources of student learning data (often in the form of exams, papers, or portfolios), the process of assessing learning may already be started in your department or college. Often this task begins with an overview of existing materials that are used to determine student learning outcomes and consideration of how these might inform discussions about enhancing what is happening in the classroom. These discussions ideally expand to the department level, but using them to better understand student learning in a single course is essential. The following questions will help to explore how existing data might be used to enhance student learning:

- Which existing outcomes are already supported by student learning data?
- Using this evidence (from the preceding question), in which areas do students seem to be reaching acceptable levels of knowledge or skill development?
- Using the existing evidence, in which areas do students seem to be lacking in acceptable levels of knowledge or skill development?

The areas that seem to show students are not learning appropriate information are important and should be targeted, since they indicate where modifications can be made to improve what students are learning and doing in the classroom.

ENGAGED STUDENTS

The term student engagement is often used in higher education literature (Bowen, 2005; Schroeder & Kuh, 2003; Kuh, 2003). Faculty frequently express the desire to engage their students more deeply with course content as part of the rationale behind revising a course. But what does this really mean? How should we go about ensuring that a revised course will better engage students? How will we know when this happens?

According to Bowen (2005), the concept of engagement can be conceptualized in four ways. The first is "student engagement with the learning process" which involves having the students become "actively involved" with the learning process rather than being the "disengaged student daydreaming in the back row" (p. 4). The questions that faculty should ask about this type of engagement involve how to get students to pay attention. What type of pedagogy can we use to get students to become engaged learners? Bowen indicates, "short-term feedback, writing across the curriculum, cooperative learning, and learning communities" (p. 4) are all pedagogical tools that can facilitate more student involvement in the process. The second type of engagement is "student engagement with the object of study" (p. 4). The third type of engagement is "student engagement with contexts of the subject of study" (p. 4). For example, what ethical issues are part of the context? Are there social issues? By using these types of context questions, faculty can help students more fully engage with the material because it is embedded within a context that is important. The fourth type of engagement is "student engagement with the human condition" (p. 4). How do students and their future fit into the content? In what ways can students use this information to better understand people? This last type of engagement draws students into the discipline by seeing the content as part of a larger whole.

Without the information that you can get from student learning outcomes data, it is difficult, if not impossible, to make changes in your course that will enhance student learning. This book is designed to help you think about the information that you have and the ways in which you use it. Most likely, you already possess important information about how much your students are learning. Using it for the purpose of redesigning your course, however, may be a new twist on thinking about this information.

As you read this book, ask yourself the following:
- What do I already know about my students?
- How do I know this information?
- Can this information be used to let me know what my students need in order to learn more or better?
- What don't I know about my students' learning?
- How can I learn which outcomes my students are not meeting?

Considering these questions will help you maximize the work you put into revising your course, regardless of the extent of the course revision. Even making minor changes in your course can result in improved student skills and learning. When you take the time and energy to make major modifications to your course, you should ensure that these changes enhance student learning. You won't know this unless you are collecting and using information on student learning. Completing the feedback loop is essential and can make your course even more meaningful to you and your students.

Chapter Two

Designing Course-Based Assessment Activities

Assessment activities that are designed to be used within the course should be created and used to find out what a student knows or can do. In other words, they should measure some type of student learning outcome. These already exist in every course—exams, papers, and projects are just a few course-based assessment activities. Using these types of student outcomes measures, you can determine what students know and assign grades to them. With enough of these activities, a faculty member can assign final course grades. This comes as no surprise to any faculty member who has taught for more than a semester in higher education. The surprise, however, comes in the knowledge that these measures, in aggregate, can also be used to revise a course. This chapter discusses methods for using existing measurements and outlines new and meaningful student activities.

Course-based student work products can help you to gather information on how well the class as a whole is doing. This double-dipping of existing assessment data means that a faculty member who is interested in redesigning a course doesn't have to do a lot of "add-ons" in order to get appropriate and significant data about how much students are learning. For many faculty members, part of the impetus for course revision is modifying the activities that students will do. This is a wonderful chance to add important and engaging learning activities that can also be used later to measure student achievement. The opportunity for creating *significant learning experiences* (Fink, 2003) within a course is an important aspect of teaching and learning and should be seriously considered as a way to increase student engagement and learning, thus adding to the usefulness of any course revision. A significant learning experience is one in which "students will be engaged in their own learning, there will be a high energy level associated with it, and the whole process will have important outcomes or results" (Fink, pp. 6-7). The results of significant learning experiences can be used to measure student achievement and to determine what students in a particular course know (or don't know). This data is essential in determining how a course should be revised. A course should not be revised once and then checked off a to-do list. Course revision should take place in a relatively continuous fashion. Each class period provides opportunities to see what is working, what should be modified, and what should be left out the next time that course is taught.

Faculty already have a wide variety of outcomes measurements for student learning. The actual type of measurement may be different across an institution or courses, but the purpose or function of this is the same: Faculty pull together information regarding how much and what type of information students are gaining over a semester or a unit (Wehlburg, 2005). The exciting part of this process for those interested in revising a course is that often the information needed already exists, and a faculty member may have years of this data—quizzes, papers, projects—on file (or in a pile!) in her or his office.

MEASURES YOU ALREADY HAVE

The abundance of existing data regarding objectives and student learning from any course can give a faculty member large amounts of information. Usually, a faculty member looks at an individual student's work over the course of a semester to assign a grade, a necessary part of the course. But faculty can relatively easily use student work products in additional ways to gather data about overall student learning patterns.

To begin, gather one set of student work from a recent semester (for example, one paper that students wrote). You have already read and graded these papers. This time, however, you will be reading them to see where students "got it" and where they fell short of meeting your objectives. Don't focus on the grade that you gave the student—that doesn't matter at this point. What you want to do is look for a pattern of information. Compare this pattern to your objectives—how close did the class (as a whole) come to meeting your requirements for student learning? Was there a group of students who did really well and a group that didn't? Can you determine anything from each group's data: Did the lower-performing group attend class irregularly? Were they non-majors? These types of questions can help you find patterns in the course.

As you look at the set of student work, make some notes involving the areas in which students seemed to fall short. You may find that a large percentage of students missed a particular part of the assignment. Even though you may have included that information on the assignment sheet (and even printed it in **bold** with underlines!), if the students still missed the information, you might be able to modify the assignment so that future students don't have the same problems. Perhaps you only need to revise the assignment sheet. Or, maybe you could add a peer-review process that students should go through before they submit the assignment.

You may also consider having a colleague read through this set of student work as a peer reviewer. If there is not a person in your department to whom you can go, is there a teaching center on your campus? If so, one of the teaching center staff members may be just the person to talk with about your course. Having another pair of eyes look at student work can give you insight into what your students are actually demonstrating, which can give you additional data to use when revising your course. It is usually best to give your peer reviewer some guidelines when looking at the set of student work. They are not regrading the individual student and they are not asked to point out errors for which you didn't deduct points. Rather, their job is to look for patterns in student understanding, sets of errors that a large percentage of students made, and/or areas of confusion that seemed to cut across much of the student work. Often with peer review, you can offer yourself as a peer reviewer, too. This ongoing collegial relationship can benefit both of you as you work to enhance student learning in your courses.

After you have looked through one complete set of student work, look back at your notes. What areas jump out at you? What content did students miss? In what areas did they fall short? What picture of student learning does this class assignment show? You are not looking for individual errors or knowledge, but overall patterns of behavior among the student work products. Your initial answers will help to guide your next steps. You will need to look for additional data in other student measures. (How to use this data is discussed further in Chapter 3.)

Continue looking for methods to assess student learning. What other work products did your students complete? Are there group projects? Papers? Video tapes? Internship journals can be a rich source of student learning data. Did you use service-learning in your course? What measures of student learning do you have for their service-learning experiences—supervisor reports or students' reaction papers? Any of these can be used to measure what students know and what skills they can demonstrate.

Measures You Can Create

As you look through the work that your students have done over the recent semester, you may find that there isn't enough information to help you determine what needs to be revised. There is only so much information that you can get from reading student responses to multiple choice tests, and if you want more data than you have, you will need to create measures that you can use; however, this isn't as overwhelming a task as it might initially sound. There are many measures that you can add to the course which will give you important and meaningful data on student learning that you can use to revise the course. A potential benefit is that just adding these new measures to your course is exactly the type of revision that you are looking for. This is an opportunity to add learning experiences to your course that will enable your students to improve their understanding of the material and give you better insight into what is working in the course. So, these *created course-based assessments* don't have to be an add-on or additional work for the course. These can become vital to the course and enrich teaching and learning.

How do you decide what measures you should create and use in your course? This question leads you back to the notes you made when looking at existing student work products. What type of information are you missing? What course objectives don't have any student work products that you can use to see what students know? Consider this a research project. What data is missing? What are the unknowns? What further information/data would you need to know more completely what students have or have not learned?

Make a list of the data that you would like to have. For example, in an educational psychology course, the instructor listed "appropriate referencing in APA style" as an objective of the course. However, when she looked back at the student work products, there was only one paper in which a student demonstrated appropriate APA-style referencing, and that paper had only three to five references. The faculty member wanted to know more about her students' knowledge and skill in using this referencing style, so she modified the existing paper assignment and increased the required number of references. She also changed the requirements about the type of references needed (e.g., additional research article references, book references, etc.). This enabled her to see how much students knew about APA-style referencing. The next semester, this faculty member found that many of her students did not have good referencing abilities. She was able to use this information to modify her course so that students could get this information. This is how using data about student learning can help to revise a course and align it with its objectives, the departmental or major objectives, and the mission of the institution. Without good student learning information, it is almost impossible to be sure that changes in the course content or pedagogy will have the desired impact.

Choose the most essential item from your list of data about student learning that is missing. Consider how a student could demonstrate their knowledge of this item to you. In the previous example, the faculty member wanted more information about her students' referencing abilities and the way to obtain that data was simply to increase the number of references that students had to complete. In another example, the instructor of a research design course found that he was missing student work that demonstrated knowledge of appropriate sampling of research subjects when he examined his objectives and compared them to the student work products. He had talked about this skill in class and there were test questions on this topic, but based on the entire class's work, he could not determine whether his students knew how to do appropriate sampling for subjects. After consulting with a colleague in a teaching center, he decided that he needed an assignment that focused on sampling. He decided to use a case study of an existing research problem and to ask his students to develop several methods for sampling that were theoretically based and ethically sound. The following semester he was able to demonstrate to himself (and to his department chair) that the majority of his students did know how to sample appropriately. This is an example of how important it is to align course objectives with the measures of student learning.

Many syllabi list several course objectives and faculty often talk to students about what they will know or be able to do as a result of the course. These objectives are important—as Laurence J. Peter has said, "if you don't know where you are going, you will probably end up somewhere else." One of several reasons to articulate course objectives is that students need to know what they will learn. If you don't have measures that align with each objective, you won't know whether students achieve the desired outcomes. Alignment is crucial and should be part of any review or revision of a course. Each objective should have a means to measure it (multiple measures are better than single measures). For example, if you want students to develop critical thinking and written communication skills, you have to provide them with the opportunity to do so. For this particular objective, you will probably have to provide several opportunities—some might be graded or given points while others might be ungraded. Even ungraded student work products can be rich sources of data about student learning.

If you haven't yet reviewed your course objectives and checked for alignment, you can do this by using a simple grid. (See figure 2.1) Begin by listing your objectives in the left column and the student work products along the top row. You can then check the boxes that correspond with each objective and student work product. If you find that there are no student work products that align with an objective, you should ask yourself, "Is this an objective that is meaningful and important to the course?" If the answer is yes, you need to develop a measurable outcome or two for that objective. If the answer is no, this is probably an objective that should be dropped from the course. If you have student work products or assignments that don't correspond to any objective, you should ask yourself why. Does this mean that the assignment does not help students achieve the goals of the course? Is it busy work? If it is an important assignment (or even if you just like it and think that it should stay), look more closely at your objectives to see where it might fit.

Figure 2.1
Aligning Course Objectives

	Work Product #1	Work Product #2	Work Product #3
Objective #1			
Objective #2			
Objective #3			

For example, in an introductory psychology course, the instructor had the students write a reaction paper based on a particularly dramatic and intense video case study of a patient with dissociative identity disorder. The reaction paper focused on the students' responses to the video, rather than on a particular theory or text-based categorization of mental disorders. At first the instructor thought that she would have to remove this assignment, because she didn't see where it fit into the overall listing of course objectives, but she really liked the assignment, because it gave students insight into this particular disorder. After consulting with a colleague from her institution's teaching center, the faculty member realized that this assignment could meet one of the objectives for the course. She then modified the wording of the objective so that it more clearly included the reflective part of the learning process. This relatively minor change in wording gave the faculty member and the students information that they needed to become more engaged with the context and the subject matter.

Writing Objectives

The more specific and accurate your course objectives are, the easier it will be to measure the skills or knowledge that you feel are important. The basic elements of a well-written objective are:

- *Content.* What do your students need to know?
- *Action.* How will students demonstrate their knowledge? Think about the behavior that you think your students should be able to show as a result of your program. Vocabulary used in this part should indicate a level in Bloom's (1956) taxonomy.
- *Content.* Under what conditions will your students demonstrate their knowledge? This focuses on where and when you would see this behavior happen. For example, you may want students to demonstrate the behavior while analyzing a written case study.
- *Performance criteria.* What standards will you use to evaluate a student's performance? What level of performance is appropriate to your department? Some may want to see test scores higher than 80 % while others always require perfect performance of the behavior.

STUDENT SATISFACTION MEASURES

Acquiring data about what a student is learning is imperative, but it is not the only type of data that can be used to make course revision decisions. Measures of student satisfaction can also be used. One caveat here: Relying too heavily on measuring student satisfaction without data on actual learning can be problematic in course revision. Of course, faculty would like for all of their students to be happy and above average, but that is not always going to be the case. Students do not always know what they will need to know for subsequent courses or for successful employment in a particular field. Faculty must create courses and learning environments that encourage students to learn and work hard. Student satisfaction should not be the outcome that we look to in order to measure our success in higher education. Measures of student learning are imperative; however, there are measures of student satisfaction that can be used, which provide rich and meaningful information that can help in the course revision process and, in turn, lead to greater student learning.

Using measures of student satisfaction can give a faculty member a great deal of information about what students perceive: What do they like? What do they think helps their learning? How are they learning? What would they like to see changed? By asking students questions such as these, you can discover what elements are hindering students in their quest for knowledge. Measures of student satisfaction are already in place on most college campuses. These include mid-semester and end-of-semester course evaluations and student responses to focus-group questions regarding the course. These data can help a faculty member decide which courses need to be revised and what portions of those courses need particular attention.

Measures of student satisfaction indicate what students think about where the course needs to be modified; however, they can only suggest aspects of the course that need to be modified. Unfortunately, this type of data is often the only source of information used by faculty to indicate what needs to be changed or modified about a course. The result of this is that courses are often made easier ("dumbed down") because students don't like certain assignments or think that the workload is too intense for the level of the course. While these perceptions may, in fact, mirror reality, they must be aligned with specific student learning outcomes measures to ensure that students are indeed learning at the level that is required or expected.

Again, alignment is important. If you can identify areas of student dissatisfaction, you can then examine them to see whether students are learning in these areas. If students demonstrate that they are learning the material, you might consider modifying the course to incorporate information gained from student satisfaction ratings—but be careful that no learning is lost. For example, in a psychology course, students expressed discontent about the structure of one of the early papers in the course. The students indicated that they did not understand the assignment and that the instructor did not give enough information to help them complete the assignment. The students further suggested that the instructor provide them with examples of the finished product. The faculty member looked closely at the students' work and determined that they were learning a great deal by working through the difficulty of writing the paper without seeing a finished product. She felt this was an important part of the process and, while frustrating, was essential to the learning outcome. She kept the assignment in her course, but she added an outline of what they would be learning from doing this project without a template to the assignment rubric to prepare students for the frustration. The following semester there were substantially fewer negative comments about the project.

In order to gather meaningful information about student satisfaction, you can use a variety of methods. One of the easiest to use is the minute paper (outlined in the following section), with which you can gather information about what students like and dislike. Ask students such questions as "What is happening in this class that is helping you to learn?" and "What is happening in this class that hinders your learning?" You can ask broad questions or detailed ones about specific assignments. Doing this several times over the course of the semester will help you develop strong qualitative evidence about what students are thinking.

SPECIFIC METHODS FOR COURSE-BASED ASSESSMENT

There are several course-based assessment instruments that you can use and modify to fit your particular course needs. These are often called *classroom assessment techniques* (CATs). CATs are methods of assessing "what students are learning in the classroom and how well they are learning it" (Angelo & Cross, 1993, p. 4). It is imperative to know how much students are learning in a course, since "teaching without learning is just talking" (p. 3).

There are hundreds of examples of classroom assessment techniques. Some take more time to administer than others, some work well online, and some can be done with almost no preparation, but they all measure some type of student learning and can be used as data for course revision and enhancement. The following are methods that you can incorporate into your course in meaningful ways that will not only enhance your understanding of student learning but will also engage your students by asking them to reflect on their own thinking.

Minute Paper

The *minute paper* technique takes up very little class time The instructor begins with a question or comment, prompting students to think about an issue and then to write a brief answer (for about a minute). Students can write their responses on index cards or a sheet of notebook paper and hand them in. This tool can be used to gather student feedback about what they like, by asking, "What is helping you to learn in this course?" It can be used to gather information about a course: "What was the most important thing you learned during this class?" or "What important question remains unanswered?" These questions can also be content specific to obtain specific information about what students know: "What are the risks of using punishment in a classroom over reinforcement?" or "Given this research question, what is a reasonable and measurable hypothesis?" or "Thinking back over the last 40 minutes in class, explain the concept of classical conditioning without using your notes."

The Muddiest Point

Related to the minute paper is the *muddiest point* (Angelo & Cross, 1993). This tool is very useful to find out which content areas are most confusing to students and what information they are missing. At the end of a class period, the faculty member asks students to respond to a question about the most confusing thing (i.e., the muddiest point) in that class period or the reading. Students can be amazingly honest about these areas and you can choose to allow students to respond to this anonymously. The student responses can be a place to start the next class period or used to send out information via email or to post to a course web page. The data gleaned from either the muddiest point or minute papers can be used in the current course and saved as data for course revision.

Just-in-Time-Teaching

Just-in-Time-Teaching (JiTT) uses before-class student responses to a set of questions. Student answers give the faculty member insight into what areas need to be focused on in class each day without having to go over information that most of the students already know. But, more than this, JiTT engages students in the material before they come to class, thus freeing up more class time to delve deeper into content and context materials. Developed by Novak and Patterson (1998), this tool can provide a great deal of data about what students know before they come into class. In addition to its intended purpose (to create lectures and course time in the current semester), this data can be used to modify the course in subsequent semesters. According to Gavrin (1996):

> Just-in-Time Teaching is a pedagogical strategy, so its learning goals are those of the instructor: mastery of the subject is always the primary concern. JiTT helps students achieve mastery by helping teachers engage students in their learning. JiTT helps instructors make the lecture setting more participatory and student cen-tered. Simultaneously, JiTT helps students stay focused and prepared to learn throughout the semester. JiTT also helps teachers identify the strengths and weakness of their students, their materials and their presentations. Thus, it helps instructors adjust the pace of the course and the quality of their resources to maximize learning. By helping teachers engage students and improve their courses, JiTT helps students learn more of the content, skills, and attitudes that faculty value. (¶ 1)

Knowing what students think they know before they come into a class can help immensely with course revision and even departmental sequencing of courses. Often students do not have the necessary prerequisite knowledge that faculty assume that they have, which can limit a student's ability and motivation to become engaged in the course and the subject matter. By knowing what students actually know, you can better provide context and information so that the time spent in class is engaging and meaningful.

Student Self-Assessment

Asking students to think about what they know (metacognition) is a means of gathering data about what students are thinking and a method to engage students in the material. According to Arnold (1992), students can reflect on why they took a particular course at the beginning of the semester, what they are learning midway through the course, and what they learned by the end of the course and how it changed their thinking: "Ultimately, all these sources of data can be examined through many different lenses" (p. 56).

One of these lenses is to view what students are thinking and consider how modifying the course content or assignments could change how they are thinking. By asking students to consider what they know and connect it with who they are and their past knowledge and experiences, students will become more engaged with the course work and content field. Reading self-reflections can provide you with rich information about who your students are, why they are taking your course, and what they hope to do with the information. This connected knowing is "personal, particular, and grounded in first-hand experience" (Belenky, Clinchy, Goldberger, & Tarule, 1997, p. 113). If your students better understand what they do know, they will be able to better express what they don't know or what might need to be altered in a course in order to enhance their learning.

Metacognitive Strategies

Metacognition is often defined as the ability to think about your own thinking. Flavell (1976) describes it in this way:

> Metacognition refers to one's knowledge concerning one's own cognitive processes or anything related to them, e.g., the learning-relevant properties of information or data. For example, I am engaging in metacognition if I notice that I am having more trouble learning A than B; if it strikes me that I should double check C before accepting it as fact. (p. 232)

Metacognition differs from self-reflection in that the learner is actively thinking about what they know and how they know that they know. It might sound confusing, but this technique works very well in class to discover what your students can do. In addition, it can become a powerful learning strategy for them in all of their courses and can enhance their ability to learn after they graduate (and what institution's mission statement doesn't include the goal of lifelong learning?). You can gather information using this strategy by asking questions such as:

• What do I know about this particular subject matter or course-related issue?
• Do I know what I need to know in order to have a more complete understanding of the topic?
• What additional information do I need to know before I would consider myself informed on this topic/issue?
• What are some strategies that I can use to learn this?
• Do I understand what I just read or heard?

By asking students to respond to these metacognitive questions, you will be providing them with the opportunity to truly think about their own knowledge. Plus, you will learn how they are processing information or assignments for your course. This data will enable you to revise assignments or create new ones so that your students will learn the material better or more clearly. For example, if your students tell you that your visual presentation of slides is distracting them from reading the text or from listening to your examples, you could modify how you present the material. Often, students are not aware of the reasons behind their seeming inability to concentrate in a course. If they are asked to think about what they are thinking they might be able to sense that a particular noise is a distraction or excessive text on a PowerPoint slide makes it difficult to follow what the faculty member is saying. This kind of data can be very useful when revising a course or making changes to particular classroom activities.

Ideally, you should create assignments and course activities that allow you to quantify individual students' knowledge (resulting in a final grade for the course) and also give you information about how much your students (as a whole) know, how they learn, and with what prior knowledge they come into your course. Knowing what should be modified in a course in order to enhance student engagement and student learning will enable you to make the best possible course revision decisions.

Chapter Three

Using Data to Enhance Innovation in Course Redesign

According to Jean Piaget (1950), intelligence is something that helps individuals adapt to a specific environment. This adaptation is very important, because without it, it would be very difficult to cope with the vast amount of information that is constantly available to us. As part of this adaptation process, humans use *schemas*. Schemas are a type of shortcut that helps us understand the world through what is expected to occur. For example, when students first walk into a classroom and see rows of chairs or desks, they normally sit down in one of them and wait for class to start. This will happen even if the rows of chairs have moved since the last time the students entered the room. In addition, a new student to the university walking into a classroom for the first time, never having seen that particular classroom, already has certain expectations about what she or he should do. Schemas are very useful, because our adaptation to the environment would suffer greatly without them and we most likely would not be able to function.

Consider this example of a schema that is so ingrained that it is difficult to see other options: A person enters a restroom in a new restaurant and walks over to the sink to wash her hands. She sees the sink and the faucet, but no handle with which to turn on the water.

How can she turn on the water and wash her hands? Has this happened to you? At first, it seems like a real problem until you realize that there is a motion sensor by the sink and that by waving your hands under the faucet the water will turn on for a predetermined time. Once you see the new option, the probability of seeing the new option increases dramatically.

Faculty also have schemas, many of which are about teaching in higher education. Some of these expectations about what occurs in a college classroom come from their experiences as students and as professors. In light of this, it makes sense that faculty teach similarly from semester to semester and course to course, and that they teach in ways that they were taught as students. Often, there isn't a lot of thought that goes into certain aspects of teaching. Of course, content changes, but many things are held constant simply because they are expected by the faculty member. For example, one faculty member has three exams per semester. When asked why, the response was, "I don't know—that is just always the way I have done it." Another faculty member who uses a lot of class time lecturing was asked why he did that. His response was, "What else would I do in class?"

These statements illustrate that it is difficult to be innovative in course design or teaching methodologies, because it is hard to see that certain aspects of the class can actually be changed. Lecturing is not the only possible use of class time, for example. When the faculty member who mostly lectured realized this, the 50 minutes of class time suddenly became an entirely open, new, and exciting space with which he could do anything (including lecturing to his students). This is the first hurdle in creating courses that use innovative techniques to enhance student learning.

And, when you include information from student learning outcomes, creating a new or different way to present information, having students apply what they know, and assessing student knowledge become much easier and more invigorating.

WHAT IS INNOVATION IN COURSE REDESIGN?

Innovation in course redesign can include many aspects of teaching and learning. Some innovations aren't really new, they are just a different way of using familiar pedagogy or technology. Some innovations are new because they are based on ever-changing technology. And, some innovations in teaching are a result of new paradigms or the allowing of new roles within the classroom. Innovation doesn't require money for new computers or new classrooms. (Of course, additional funding can help to support innovation, but it isn't always necessary.) The purpose of this section is to outline some innovative ways to approach teaching and learning. As with this entire book, the end result of these pedagogical approaches should be increased student learning. While many faculty may have started using PowerPoint or other presentation software primarily because it was "new" or "exciting," innovative course design should be aimed toward enhancing what students are learning and increasing their engagement in the classroom and with the material.

Students' Prior Learning

Students walk into a classroom with prior learning about the specific discipline of the course, expectations about the particular faculty member and the course, and information from their general experiences that will impact their learning. The new learning that a student does is determined by what the student already knows and has experienced. In this way, all new learning is constructed by the student. This explains, in part, why after hearing or reading information, some students don't understand it in the same way as others. Their prior knowledge was different and, thus, the construction of new knowledge is different. Students may actually perceive the information (new knowledge) differently because of their existing structure of information. Marilla Svinicki (1993) uses an example of the word "cardinal" in a mini-experiment. What do you think of when you hear that word? For those interested in sports (or those who live in St. Louis), baseball might come to mind. Others might think of birds or even the Roman Catholic church. What you think of demonstrates the structure of information that you have and how the context of learning new information is based on the perception that occurs when that new information is presented. Faculty may use terminology that students don't understand, or they may ask students to read information for which a particular student doesn't have the prerequisite skills or knowledge with which to understand the new information.

Because of the need for context and correct perception in order to learn new information appropriately, the way in which information is presented can impact how a student organizes new information that she or he has learned. If the context is incorrect, the structure and correctness of the new information may be completely wrong. If, for example, students in an introductory astronomy course have a prior belief that the weather is warmer in the summer because the earth gets closer to the sun during that time (rather than the tilt of the earth's axis), these students will have a difficult time understanding much of what is to follow in the course about planetary motion. In this way prior learning can negatively impact students' acquisition of new knowledge.

Given the importance of a student's prior knowledge, what can be done to innovatively enhance a course? What can be added or modified to enhance student learning? To incorporate the role of prior knowledge, review information at the beginning of class that is necessary for students to know and understand. Alternatively, you could ask students to do the review for the class, ensuring that the review is based on correct information. Simply asking students to compare new concepts that they have learned with old concepts that are correct can improve student learning. Another simple, yet innovative technique is to ask students to reflect upon past courses that they have taken or experiences that they have had that are related to the new information. This will help students as they add the new information to their existing cognitive structure. And, if you are able to monitor what students are saying, you can correct misinformation before it becomes constructed incorrectly.

Just being aware that students often enter your courses with incorrect and missing information can be enough to change the way you present information and assess student understanding. Knowing that students will construct the information that you give them rather than taking it as a whole may modify your approach to use of class time. The reality is that human science has not yet discovered how we actually learn and why some learn differently and at different rates from others. Halpern and Hakel (2002) claim that even though there has been some recent growth in knowledge about how we learn, "very little of this basic knowledge has been translated into practice, many research questions that are critically important for directing educational reform remain unanswered, and few in the scientific community have been actively involved in the efforts to reform higher education" (p. 1); however, we do know, "the interface between prior experience or learning and its effect on new or novel situations is a crucial area" (Macaulay & Cree, 1999, p. 185). Thus, it is important to take into account the prior learning that students bring to your classes. Use this information to involve students actively in learning and in checking their prior and new learning. In this way you can be innovative without making radical changes to your course while still enhancing student learning.

Team-Based Learning, Group Activities, and Collaborative Learning

For some students, learning has been a solitary task. They may sit alone to read the text, they may even study alone. They take their own notes in class and use them to prepare for exams. When they take exams, their grade depends on how prepared they are and how well they can respond, individually, to the test items. In contrast, many students are very comfortable working in groups. They may already rely on peer groups for many decisions in their lives, and they are used to working with peers on class projects. By incorporating team learning and group work into your class, you are engaging students in collaborative ways with each other and with the material. In addition, you may be preparing them for post-college employment opportunities, since many employers are now looking to hire students who have good team skills.

There is a difference between *collaborative learning*, *cooperative learning*, and *team-based learning*, even though these terms are often used interchangeably. Collaborative learning is designed so that students work together to explore a topic in depth or discuss a lecture issue. Cooperative learning is a specific type of collaborative learning, in which students work on structured activities. Team-based learning is also a type of collaborative learning. Teams are groups of students that form and stay together for a longer term, often throughout an entire semester. Part of the team's work may be on a particular project, but it can also be that teams discuss lecture issues and discussion questions.

The difficulty for many faculty with team-based learning and group assignments is that they can be difficult to grade. How do you assign individual scores or points to something that was done by a group? How do you make it fair to those students within the group who may have done more than their "fair share?" What about those students who do not work to the level of their peers? It can be difficult to ensure fairness, but there are many methods and models that can be used to enhance learning and provide appropriate individual grades. Some assignments are worked on as a group, but each student submits his or her own report and gets an individual grade for that work. In other situations, there is one group project and all students within that group get the same grade, regardless of how much actual work they put into the project. Another way to grade group work is to combine the individual work and the group process: Have students submit a group project and ratings of each other in terms of the amount of work that they did. Students may then receive two grades—one collective grade for the project and an individual grade from group members.

Another reason faculty avoid using group work is the potential for less coverage of material in the classroom. Because student discussion and group work take longer than a lecture on almost any topic, there will be less time in class to cover material. However, when students are actively engaged in material and are discussing it and applying it to problems or cases, they learn the material better. This means that even though less content is mentioned during class time, students are learning more. Also, keep in mind that students do not only learn during class time. They can learn prior to class by doing readings or researching a topic. When students come to class prepared to apply what they know, the amount of learning increases, students are engaged in the material, and they often report higher levels of satisfaction with the course. Just because a faculty member said something in class does not mean that students learned it. Faculty statements are not the only prerequisite to knowledge acquisition on the part of the student. However, creating an environment in which student learning is the goal can make a huge difference in how much students learn and the methods that are used.

The use of collaborative learning can benefit all members of a class or group. Students learn content from each other and they must teach content to others. Group work and collaborative learning techniques can allow for active learning on a particular topic. When students have to think and respond to a group (rather than just write down lecture notes) they learn the material in richer ways. Even asking full-class discussion questions can get some students to begin thinking about issues. But asking students to do actual work within a small group gives them greater opportunity to think and share their knowledge and insights. In addition, when groups are working on a project, they may work harder so that they don't let the other team members down. While there will always be a few social loafers, the majority of students will work within a group to create learning for the entire group if the assignment provides them with that opportunity.

The design of a group or team assignment is crucial in terms of determining the amount of work that students will put into the task. The impetus for working hard on a project comes in part from the weight of the assignment. Is the work appropriate to the number of points that they will get for successful completion of the project? Or, will students see the group assignment as busy work or something that isn't going to do them any good in the long run? Creating effective and innovative group assignments requires some upfront work and preparation. But once these are created, they can be used again and again with modifications made after each instance based on student learning and faculty observations about the technique. The following are some examples of collaborative learning that can be implemented in almost any class.

Roundtable discussion. This technique works very well when the goal is to brainstorm ideas and solutions. The faculty member poses a specific question. This question should have several correct or appropriate answers. Each group has one pen and one piece of paper. The first student writes a response and says it out loud, the second does the same, and it goes around the table until time is called. Most instructors allow a student to pass at any point if they don't have anything specific to add to the list. Students are not to critique any responses during the brainstorming time period. After the time is up, students might post their lists, or each group might begin by looking at their own lists in a search of a solution or answer to the original question.

Paired annotations. In this collaborative learning technique, students are placed in pairs and each pair reads an assigned article or chapter. Each student responds to the reading as outlined by the professor. For example, they might critique the specific research design used in the article or list the major points of the article. Students read and discuss each other's responses and then, working together, prepare a single composite annotation that responds to the assignment.

Guided reciprocal questioning. In this activity, the faculty member first presents information in the form of a reading assignment, a lecture, or any other method. Groups are then given question stems based on the readings. A question stem is the first part of a question. For example:

• Using collaborative learning techniques, how can students learn _____ ?
• How does _____ impact _____ ?
• What is a new example of _____ ?
• How does group work _____ ?

These types of question stems may have many responses. Student groups take these question stems and create questions and answers to those questions. At the end of the time given, these questions can be used to stimulate class discussion. The goal of the activity is to have students think about the content in several ways; creating a meaningful question requires that students have a full understanding of the issues and the content. It is amazing to see the types of questions that students can develop using this technique!

Problem-Based Learning

Using problem-based learning (PBL) to enhance a student's active experience with material can increase student learning in novel ways. PBL is a teaching method that asks students to solve real-world style problems, most often in groups. Students are used to coming into college classes, sitting down, and taking notes, but when they are given a problem with no solutions and asked to develop solutions on their own, they are pushed into finding out additional information that goes beyond the textbook. They then apply that information to the particular problem at hand, discuss potential solutions with their group members, and synthesize the possible solution strategies into the one that they think will work.

One of the interesting aspects of incorporating problem-based learning into your courses is that the content should not be presented before the problem. Instead, only the problem (one that is complex and as much like the real world as possible) should be given to students. While students often initially find this frustrating because they don't know the "right" answer and they don't know whether information they find will be relevant or completely meaningless to the particular problem, it is an excellent method of getting students to think critically and analytically about a complex issue.

Problems should be chosen carefully. They should be sufficiently complicated, reflecting the difficult and sometimes messy elements of real problems. Here is an example of a problem used in an introductory art history class:

> You have been hired as consultants for a major motion picture. Although the story, set in ancient Greece (c.425 B.C.), is fictional, the director wants every detail in the film to be as

historically accurate as possible. Part of the action will take place around a temple. Your task is to determine what this temple should be like—including the interior, the exterior, the immediate vicinity, and the activities in and around the temple. If possible, recommend a location (or locations) where the filming of the temple scene could take place. Include notes about what, if any, aspects of the setting would need to be altered—either physically or through special effects—in order to be accurate (Miller, 1996, ¶ 1).

As you can see in this example, the problem is not clear-cut and there are numerous possible solutions. Students must research temples in ancient Greece in a variety of ways. They must work together to make decisions about what they will recommend, and they must have a large set of knowledge about this time period, temple architecture, and temple activities.

Case Studies

A case study is a story or detailed scenario that provides context and a rich and complex description of an event. One of the difficulties of using full cases in your classes is that doing it well requires advance preparation by you and your students. For those students who don't prepare, the activity just becomes another discussion rather than an application of learned material to a case, therefore it is essential that students are prepared to discuss the case study. They must read it and think about it prior to class. Some faculty provide discussion questions to help students consider the case. Other cases end in a "now what?" way and the questions for thinking about the case are relatively obvious. For either method, explain your expectations to students when preparation is crucial.

To begin, you must decide which case to use. There are many sources of good cases that are discipline based—many textbooks now come with case studies and there are case-study texts that only contain cases in a particular discipline. In addition, real-life examples of cases can be used from the news, local newspapers, or other events.

When choosing a case, Herreid (1997/1998) suggests that you look for one with some level of controversy. He adds, "a good case tells a story"(p. 163), is relatively recent, is one in which the students care about the main characters, and has dialogue. This, Herreid points out, causes students to better understand the human nature of the main characters in the case. In addition to these, a good case should serve the educational function of the course and require that specific issues or dilemmas be solved.

Once the case is chosen, you must set the stage for discussing the case. This doesn't have to be a dramatic introduction, but you should probably say a few words about it before jumping into to a specific question. As case study discussions often occur within the entire class setting, the first question normally comes from the instructor. This first question is important because it begins the entire case discussion. You want to make it open enough to encourage participation, but not so open that you lose the starting point and veer off into many different directions. It is very appropriate to ask simple questions such as "who are the main characters?" or "what seems to be the main issue here?" As the discussion begins, encourage as many students to participate as possible. Sometimes the discussion takes off and students respond to each other and your role is minimized. Often, however, (especially early in the semester when students aren't yet used to case discussions) you will need to ask follow-up questions and questions that will move the discussion forward. Ensure that students are all focused on the discussion. As the discussion gets more involved it is possible that students will try to interrupt each other or have side conversations (even on-task ones) with their classmates. It is up to you to keep the discussion moving in the direction that will be most educationally beneficial to the students. Sometimes that means allowing a tangent to become more prominent, sometimes it may mean that you have to redirect a student to focus more on a particular issue.

As the discussion time ends, it is important to remember that you may not have come to a unanimous class decision on what should happen next in the case. Students may disagree with each other or there may be more information that they want to have before they make a final decision. That is just fine. It may be that the discussion process itself was the point—students thought about the information that they already had and applied it in ways that made them reassess their previous beliefs or understanding of a particular issue. If that is the case, then there is no real need for closure with a final decision. Sometimes, though, you may want students to finalize their decisions. You could ask students to write their individual decisions and hand them in to you or share them with their small groups or the class. If there isn't clear consensus, you might consider having students vote on the decision that they would make. If students on the losing side of the vote want to write a minority statement, that can work well, too, since it can enhance their learning and motivation for the task. This technique gets students to apply information to real world issues and can be an engaging way to get them to learn more about the content than a traditional lecture might do.

Discussion

Several of the previous innovative techniques have involved discussion—both small group and whole class. In-class discussions don't always have to be formal, planned activities. Some are formal by their nature. For example, case studies generate formal discussion. The purpose of that portion of class is to have a discussion that will cover relatively specific topics. Introducing formal and planned discussion questions in your class can add active learning to your class without adding a great deal of time and effort on your part.

There are several ways that you can incorporate class discussion into your course. All revolve around a central premise: You need to ask your class a question and wait for them to answer it. Often faculty ask questions without waiting for students to answer. These become rhetorical questions and don't usually prompt students to think about the question and formulate an answer. But, by asking a question and then waiting for a response (and you will get one!), you are putting students into a thinking mode rather than a listening mode.

Informal discussions can occur spontaneously. Sometimes they happen when a student asks a question about something that was just said in class. You can take this question and turn it around to the class. Ask someone else to respond to the question. Ask for ideas. In addition to having a student ask a question, an issue may come up that causes you to want to ask a question. Perhaps you want to check to see if the students understood the content that you just presented, or maybe you want them to think more deeply about a current event or a video that you just showed in class. By asking them something as simple as "what do you think?" or "why did this happen?" you are encouraging them to actively participate in class and to think more deeply about their own knowledge.

Formal discussions are also excellent methods to get students to think about, apply, analyze, and evaluate information. There are varying levels of formality in using discussions. For example, one psychology faculty member adds specific discussion questions to her PowerPoint presentations. She pauses in her lectures and has students respond to the questions. This method tends to result in a short discussion. If, however, the class period is going to have a longer discussion, then the planning for that will reflect the difference. When asking students to prepare specifically for a discussion, they must know what to read and it is often helpful to give them some of the discussion questions ahead of time. This allows them to begin to think more deeply about the particular topic and to prepare for the discussion. This also helps students know what the objective of the discussion is. For example, you may want students to focus on the subject matter or you may want them to apply the subject matter to a specific situation.

As you prepare for a discussion, consider the physical setup of your classroom, because different settings can impact the climate of the classroom. It is much more difficult to have full class discussions when students are looking at each others' backs than if they are in a circle and can see their classmate's faces. Also, consider the rules that you have for discussion. Some faculty choose to put these expectations into their syllabus. Others may explain them at the beginning of each discussion (and some do both!). It is always easier to set the rules before the discussion gets started. Once a discussion has begun and someone violates a rule (interrupts a classmate, for example), it is much more difficult to implement the rule.

As the discussion progresses, your role will change. You may start as the "direct questioner" but you may move more into the background of the discussion as it moves forward and students take center stage. You may need to step in to summarize particular issues that have been discussed, identify key points made by students, or ask for clarification of student comments. If it seems that the discussion is not moving forward or has hit "the wall," you may consider asking students to think about the question and write down their answers. They can then share them with a partner and you can ask for responses to the question after they have had time to briefly discuss with their partners. This "think, pair, share" technique can help to get students involved with the material and can help to move the discussion forward. "Discussion is a particularly wonderful way to explore supposedly settled questions and to develop a fuller appreciation for the multiplicity of human experience and knowledge" (Brookfield & Preskill, 1999, p. 3).

Portfolios

Using portfolios in your classes requires students to prepare and collect several artifacts or work products and combine them in a single space in order to represent a sample of student knowledge or performance. In the past, portfolios have been paper-based, but now many portfolios are kept in digital format. Both electronic and paper portfolios hold several uses for teaching and learning. For example, a portfolio might contain a student's best work over the course of the semester and be used at the end of the semester for part of that student's grade. Or, a portfolio can be used to demonstrate a work in progress to indicate the process that a student went through to complete a project. One of the important aspects of a portfolio is that it highlights the role of the student in the instructional process. A portfolio's contents can be outlined by the faculty member, but the artifacts within it are up to the student to choose and to create.

Portfolios don't just have to be the work of a single student; they can be used as part of a group assignment or a team project. Students can comment on each other's work within a single portfolio or across several portfolios. As part of the process of collecting information on what will go into a portfolio, students are often required to reflect on the work that it contains. At one institution, students create portfolios that demonstrate knowledge across the general education program and, at the senior year, each student must read through all of the contents of his or her portfolio and reflect on what has been learned over the past 4 years. This reflection process allows students to be observers of their own work and to think about it in ways that they may not have done before. Portfolios can provide innovative learning opportunities for students and can also be used to collect data on how much students are learning in a course.

Web-Enhanced Courses

In a web-enhanced course the faculty and students meet face-to-face in a traditional setting, but the course includes web-technology that supports its design and delivery. There are many for-profit course management programs (e.g., Blackboard, WebCT, and eCollege) and some that are designed in-house for specific institutions. In addition, many faculty create web pages to augment their courses. There are elements to many of the web-enhanced systems that can be used to structure innovative learning opportunities for students. Some of the basic, static aspects of these web pages include the ability to post course documents such as the syllabus or assignment sheets. Students tend to respond well to having these items online.

The static "storing" of documents is a wonderful addition to a course, but there are several more interactive aspects to having a web site. A virtual classroom gives faculty and students additional opportunities for interaction. Chat rooms, threaded discussions, and journaling are just some of the many options available through course management systems and web pages. As technology continues to grow, these interactive opportunities will also change. How you decide to use these new and ever-changing technologies will be up to you. Some faculty have become very interested in staying cutting edge while others progress at different rates. The important part of using technology for teaching and learning is that it must actually support teaching and learning. Before incorporating a new technology, ask, "how will this help students learn?" or, "what impact will this have on the class and learning?" There are many types of technologies and some work better than others in specific circumstances. Remember, low-tech chalk is a great tool, too! Having a class with a web page and students interacting with each other online can be a wonderful and innovative enhancement to the class as long as students are learning the content and meeting course outcomes. If you decide that adding a blog or a Wiki to your course will enhance learning or keep students engaged, by all means try it and see! The data that you collect will enable you to determine how that technique is working and can guide the decision-making for any revising of your course.

GETTING INNOVATIVE

As you look at the student learning and other forms of data from previous semesters, consider incorporating some innovative aspects into your course. What you decide to do is completely up to you—but remember that you can always add in a teaching technique or a case discussion to see how it works. And, if it does seem to increase student learning or engagement, you can add more to the course for the next semester. Trying something new can be difficult, but the potential benefits are well worth the extra effort! For example, one faculty member completely redesigned her whole introductory religion course to move away from lecture and incorporate team-based learning and group discussions. At the end of the semester, she was pleased with parts of the course, but felt as if she had added in too many quizzes. So, she made some additional modifications and is now very pleased with the results of her work.

Innovative changes to any course are the result of planning, decision-making based on information, and a certain amount of courage. The potential benefits to the increased student learning, enhanced engagement, and the enjoyment of teaching and learning, however, make the work well worth the time and energy.

Chapter Four

Rethinking Teaching
and Learning

"If a tree falls in the forest and no one is there to hear it, does it still make a sound?" This is probably one of the most often used philosophical questions around. There are, of course, many answers to this question and the answers given hinge on specific definitions of words. What does "sound" mean? What does "hearing" mean? Part of the joy of discussing this, or any philosophy, is that there is not one "correct" answer, but the process of the discussion provides opportunities for learning and exploring new concepts. The same concept can be used with teaching: "If a faculty member is lecturing to a group of students and no learning occurs, is the faculty member teaching?"

This twist on the old question is an intriguing prompt for any group of educators. What does teaching mean? Can you teach without learning? Can you learn without teaching? According to Angelo and Cross (1993), "learning can and often does take place without the benefit of teaching . . . but there is no such thing as effective teaching in the absence of learning" (p. 3). If this is true, then the answer to the above philosophical question is "no." Lecturing without fostering student learning is not teaching, it is a monologue on the part of the faculty member. So, what is good teaching? One way to look at it is that the effectiveness of teaching can only be measured by looking at how much students learn. The more learning that takes place, in theory, the better the teaching. If only it were that simple. There are many ways to measure student learning (faculty measure this all the time when assigning grades), but these measurements are rarely used in deciding what effective teaching is. Instead, many universities use other methods for measuring teaching (Chism, 1999).

Other methods for measuring quality of teaching have, unfortunately, not been as well validated. One of these methods is student evaluations of teaching. Almost every post-secondary institution uses these measures and they often focus on student satisfaction or perceptions. While there are studies that document a positive correlation between student learning and student evaluations of teaching, they are not a measure of student learning and should not be used as such. These evaluations often ask students to consider issues that may be important, but are not always essential. One example of this can be seen in questions on class or teacher organization: "On a scale of 1–5, how organized was the class time for this course?" Students can certainly be good judges of organization and time management within a class, but a low score on organization does not necessarily equate to poor teaching. For example, a faculty member in philosophy got good overall teaching evaluations over several semesters and student comments were mostly positive, but a recurrent theme was that her course was not well organized. She decided to ask more detailed questions to discover what students meant by this, because her judgment was that her course was very well organized. She asked a colleague to come in and observe her class. What the colleague discovered were students who were very interested in the course, asked excellent questions, and had obviously done the reading prior to class. This faculty member was an incredible storyteller and would explain the subject matter in a way that drew students into the content and engaged them in thinking about philosophy. They were so interested in what she was saying and what their classmates were asking, that the notes students took in class were fragmented. So, at the end of the semester or before a unit exam, students would look back over their notes and not see any organization. Their response was that it must be that the faculty member was not organized during class time. It became a simple matter of writing a brief outline on the board before class time to guide the students through the class time. The comments about disorganization decreased, while student learning and engagement remained high. And, the faculty member was able to maintain her teaching style without going to something more structured (using presentation software, for example).

Student evaluations can be useful measures of what is engaging students and how they feel about a particular course or faculty member. But, in most cases, they are not direct measures of student learning and should not be the only data used for course revision (or any other academic decisions that involve teaching and learning quality, for that matter).

STUDENT-CENTERED TEACHING

The teaching and learning paradigm has transitioned from teaching in a teacher-centered way to something more student centered. Teacher-centered teaching is that which is focused mainly on what the faculty member believes needs to be taught using the pedagogy that the faculty member finds most comfortable. However, with the research on learning styles, attention has been focused on the differences in how students learn. Interestingly, the learning style of most faculty is very different from the learning styles of most students, and faculty usually teach in the same ways that they were taught (Halpern & Hakel, 2002). To focus on what the students in a particular course might need in order to learn is generally considered to be student centered. It does not mean that a course is made easier to make the students "happy" or to make them "satisfied" about the course experiences. Rather, it is an attempt to engage the students in the content and facilitate the learning that they must do. They are not "buckets to be filled" with knowledge, but candles which need lighting (Yeats). Once the focus is taken away from what the faculty member feels he or she must cover, the needs of the students can take precedence. This is a crucial shift in thinking and one that is necessary for truly meaningful course redesign. Faculty generally teach in the way that would work for them if they were a student, but most students are not going to become faculty members and they have different learning styles and prior experiences that should be taken into consideration in the course:

> The idea of focusing on learning rather than teaching requires that we rethink our role and the role of students in the learning process . . . we must challenge our basic assumptions about how people learn and what the roles of a teacher should be. (Huba & Freed, 2000, p. 3)

STUDENT ENGAGEMENT

When a course experience engages a student in the content and in the context of a course, that student is drawn into the course. Many faculty felt this way when they took courses in their major (as an undergraduate), and especially when they were in graduate school. There was an almost single-minded approach to learning something. It didn't matter how many hours it took, what the process involved, or even how many points were assigned. The learning of something was simply the most important thing to do. Graduate students who are involved in dissertation research, for example, may spend hundreds of hours in a lab or in the library studying a particular area. They are engaged in learning for the sake of understanding and meaningfulness. Contrast that with an undergraduate student who is taking a course because it is a required course outside their major. This undergraduate student will probably do the least amount of work possible in order to get the needed grade. Questions such as "will this be on test?" are common. What the student is really saying is "tell me if you think this is important because if it isn't I am not going to spend any time learning it." Students who are not engaged in the content may also want to know how many points an assignment is worth. What they may be saying in this case is, "are the points assigned for this enough points for me to care about how well I do the assignment? Are the points worth the amount of time that it looks like I will spend on it?" While there will always be questions like these (even in courses where the students are engaged), by getting the students interested, curious, or emotionally concerned about a topic, a teacher can create an environment that will lead to increased learning and internalization of the subject matter. In addition, students will be more likely to take the lead in discussions and will be much more apt to read material before class. This may sound like educational nirvana and something that is almost impossible to do, but it can be done.

While there are situations in which a student can become emotionally involved in a situation without truly understanding it, this type of engagement is generally short lived and doesn't lead to long term learning or engagement over time in the subject. So in most cases, becoming engaged in a subject matter means that a student has some significant level of competence in the basic information of the particular subject matter. Without a basic understanding of content, it is impossible to become engaged in the material:

> To develop competence in the area of inquiry, students must: (a) have a deep foundation of factual knowledge, (b) understand facts and ideas in the context of a conceptual framework, and (c) organize knowledge in the ways that facilitate retrieval and application. (Bransford, Brown, & Cocking, 2000, p. 16)

For many college-level courses, faculty assume that students come in with foundational knowledge. Institutions have prerequisites for many courses. Unfortunately, students may not actually come into class on the first day with all of the information, knowledge, or skills that it is assumed they have. One method that is often used to discover the preexisting knowledge of students is to give a pretest or to ask students to demonstrate particular skills. This can work very well in a language course—students can demonstrate fluency at a particular level of a language and can then be put into the appropriate course. In other classes, the material that is expected to be known isn't as easily measured. For example, in the video, *A Private Universe* (Harvard-Smithsonian Center for Astrophysics, 1987), the incorrect preexisting beliefs of middle school students about what makes the Earth warm during the summer and cold during the winter get in the way of learning the correct explanations. Even when students are taught the correct explanations for seasonal warming and cooling, they are not able to grasp or fully understand the correct conceptual theory because their preexisting belief is so all-encompassing. They believe that the earth is warmer in the summer because the Earth is closer to the sun. If we move our hand closer to a heat source (for example, a light bulb), our hand gets hotter. Therefore, according to this naïve and incorrect theory, when it gets warmer on Earth in the summer, we must be getting closer to a heat source, the sun. As the teacher describes indirect and direct light waves from the sun as being responsible for the heating and cooling, the students try to put that within what they already "know." But, since it doesn't fit, they go back to what they originally believed. (Interestingly, some of the students tried very hard to "fit" the new information into their old conceptual framework and ended up with some very bizarre descriptions of a curly-cue path that the Earth takes around the sun.) Students, and humans in general, will create explanations for things that they don't understand. It is very difficult to tear down these mental constructions and replace them with the correct framework—but it can be done.

Students need to "learn with understanding" (Bransford, Brown, & Cocking, 2000, p. 16). This will enable them not to just learn facts (rote memorization) but to incorporate these facts into a larger, meaningful conceptual framework. Faculty need to be aware of the fact that students will not always come into a course with the prerequisite knowledge, and even worse, may come in with incorrect preexisting belief systems that will make learning in that course much more difficult. To create an environment in which students can "learn with understanding," faculty need to intentionally ask students for information on what they are thinking. This is often done in the form of a quiz or exam, but by using this type of summative assessment, it is too late for the student to correct the information and use it for the course. By building formative assessment opportunities into the course, the students will know what they know and the faculty member can make sure that the appropriate theoretical framework is in place for them. Getting students to verbalize information, think and respond to case studies, or discuss complex questions are all ways to get students to think about their own thinking. These will encourage students to question their own knowledge and become more reflective about their own thinking. This reflective thinking is a wonderful skill that students should have, but even more important is the opportunity to get feedback about their thinking from other students and from their instructor. Without a solid foundational knowledge of information, it is difficult to become engaged in a course. So, by monitoring student understanding and checking the conceptual framework, a faculty member can guide students when they are starting to veer away from accepted thinking patterns: "The use of frequent formative assessment helps make students' thinking visible to themselves, their peers, and their teacher" (Bransford, Brown, & Cocking, 2000, p. 19).

Developing a usable and correct conceptual framework also means that students will need more than a superficial "covering" of information. When students in a course are not asked to do more than remember a few specific dates or memorize a formula, they are not going to become engaged in the material. For example, when teaching a statistics course, a faculty member began the course with concepts rather than formulas. The students were asked to look at a proposed research study and ask questions about what could be done with data. In small groups, students were able to outline how the sample might be different from the population and what additional information they needed. Only later on were they given the exact formulas to use. The emphasis was on *why* to use a particular formula rather than on the formula itself. Students were able to first build a conceptual framework and then add the formulas to the framework at a later time. As students were working through the proposed research study, they were able to check their understanding and clarify things when they didn't fully understand. They were free to question their own knowledge and not worry about being wrong. As a matter of fact, being "wrong" for students in this course was seen as a positive thing because they were checking their own understanding. The faculty member was able to circulate through the class and hear what students were saying, and add corrections and modifications as she went. At the end of the semester, students in this course responded very positively on course evaluations and entered the senior capstone course much better prepared to design and complete a research study.

Formative assessment methods "permit the teacher to grasp the students' preconceptions, understand where the students are in the 'developmental corridor' from informal to formal thinking and design instruction accordingly" (Bransford, Brown, & Cocking, 2000, p. 24). This focus on student learning is student-centered teaching. Every class may have to be taught a little differently and the faculty member must be flexible enough to choose pedagogical methods that will meet the needs of students in that class. This does not mean, however, that every class period is unplanned or unstructured. Rather, the general outline of the class is set (and, in the case of teaching multiple sections, can be identical). But within that preset structure, there may be different explanations or examples that the faculty member can use to make learning occur.

TRANSFER OF LEARNING

Once students are engaged in a particular course, they develop a new perspective or lens through which to view other material. This new perspective will show up in other courses. Students will begin to transfer learning from one course to others. Within the major this is essential, but is often unplanned. Departmental curricular design assumes that students will learn from the "intro" course and then use that material in successive courses. However, this is not always the case. In any particular course, it is important to intentionally design an environment that encourages transfer of learning into the course from other—previous or concurrent—courses and prepares the student to use knowledge and skills gained for later application (in college and, more importantly, for a lifetime).

How can a faculty member support a learning environment that will engage students and encourage transfer of learning? Part of the answer to this question is already embedded in teaching: "All new learning involves transfer based on previous learning" (Bransford, Brown, & Cocking, 2000, p. 53). Given this, students are already transferring in information or skills that they have previously learned. This makes the task much easier, since students are already doing this. As students are presented with new information, they store that new information within a previously learned context. If the previous learning is incorrect, the new learning will not "fit" with other information that will be learned in the course and the student will probably end up confused and unengaged with the material or the course. But, if the new learning fits in well with correct and appropriate prior knowledge, the student is well on her or his way to new learning that can be used within the new course. The previous knowledge is learning that is being transferred into the current class—transfer of learning is occurring. But this is often where the transfer of learning ends, at least on the part of the faculty member. Students may not be asked to actively take information from other courses. Sometimes this is because the faculty member is not sure that students actually have the prerequisite knowledge, but it often seems to be simply because the intentional methodology of using prior knowledge to engage students in new content is not considered.

In order to transfer learning into a course, students must have learned the material in the first place. This makes sense, but students are often asked to memorize information rather than to develop a deeper and more meaningful understanding of information (Halpern & Hakel, 2002). Graesser, Person, and Hu (2002) outline several methods for intentionally creating a learning atmosphere that will encourage "deep comprehension." The first of these is to have the students construct their own explanations regarding new information or ideas. Having students creating these explanations means that they are not only memorizing facts, they are understanding them. Asking "why" or "what if" are some of the prompts that students can use to begin their explanations.

Graesser, Person, and Hu also suggest that faculty should challenge a student's belief system and previous knowledge: "Imagine walking into a classroom and proclaiming that today's students are prone to follow fads, that rap music is dead, or that global warming is not a significant problem to worry about" (p. 38). What do you think a student's response will be? Most likely, these types of statements will force a student to look back at previous knowledge (transferring learning in from other contexts) and create an argument against the faculty member's statement. Not only does this engage a student in the content, but it requires and supports the transfer of learning from another context.

Creating this "cognitive disequilibrium" often causes a student to think more deeply about a particular topic and may set the stage for engagement and enhanced learning. An undergraduate student in a social psychology course frequently asked questions of the faculty member that indicated her disagreement with the theories presented in the course. Rather than regularly debating with this student, the faculty member responded with questions. "What differences do you see in the behaviorist approach to this situation? How would a Freudian theorist explain this particular event?" When asked these types of questions, the student was forced to look more closely at similarities and differences among several theories. This involved significant transfer of learning into the course and an increased amount of engagement with the material. Essentially, the student was trying to argue the weakness of social psychology as a method to explain human behavior, but had to study the theory in much more detail in order to make a convincing argument. The student ended up with a major in psychology that was strongly influenced by the theories within social psychology.

Another aspect to enhancing the transfer of learning is to ensure that when the learning occurs it is not "overly contextualized" (Bransford, Brown, & Cocking, 2000, p. 53). Research supports the practice of using more types of representations of problems that are more abstract (Singley & Anderson, 1989). For example, in an accounting course, students regularly reported frustration with the course and the instructor, because the test items were very different from the homework problems. To the faculty member, this did not make sense as he explained that the homework problems were actually much more difficult and complex than the exam questions. The students, however, only learned one way to solve one particular type of problem. When the test item seemed to be a different type of problem (even though it was not), students without a thorough understanding of the material could not solve the exam problems. Those students who could solve the exam problems, however, reported that the exam questions were easier than the homework problems. These students had a better and more complete understanding of the material. By changing the types of homework problems so that they included several different types of problems and shifting the focus away from inputting numbers into a formula, the faculty member was able to increase student learning. The majority of the students are better at transferring knowledge from one type of problem to another within a course. These students will also be much better prepared for the next course in the accounting sequence—they will be able to transfer knowledge into their new courses by using a more abstract conceptualization of problem solving in accounting rather than the traditional solving of particular homework problems.

THE "GUIDE ON THE SIDE"

In rethinking teaching and learning, many in higher education are moving away from the lecture-and-listen-only class period as the primary means of conducting a course. Even large classes with hundreds of students can benefit from a mix of pedagogical teaching methods. In moving to a more student-centered approach to teaching, many faculty are becoming interested in incorporating the teacher-as-facilitator (the "guide on the side") conceptualization of teaching. This movement away from being a "sage on the stage" allows for the integration of new teaching methods such as small group work, teaming, discussions, and experiential learning. By recognizing that students learn best when they create their own explanations, construct their own knowledge within the context of their prior learning, and transfer in learning from previous courses, a faculty member can easily see how facilitating learning can be a very powerful and engaging tool. But the change to this style of teaching and learning can be difficult. Faculty often have serious concerns about how students will learn if the faculty member doesn't cover all of the information. Students do not always come to class prepared and with sufficient knowledge to think deeply about a particular subject. How, then, can this work?

ACTIVE LEARNING

When using active learning, students are involved in some type of content-specific behavior other than listening. This could be cooperative learning, discussions, writing responses, or any teaching and learning practice that causes the student to act. Moving to incorporate active learning does not have to be a huge change in pedagogy for a particular faculty member. In one research study (Ruhl,

Hughes, & Schloss, 1987), an instructor stopped lecturing about every 15 minutes and asked students to work in pairs to rewrite their notes for 2 minutes. Amazingly, on a free recall exam following the class period, students performed significantly better in courses where the instructor paused than in courses with no pauses. And, even more important, increases in learning were still apparent 12 days after the lecture. In other words, by taking a mere 6 minutes out of lecturing and asking students to actively think and write about their notes, learning was enhanced. This increased learning may not have been due only to the 2-minute active learning times, the shortened lectures may have also played a role in student learning. This very simple change can be incorporated into almost any course that is primarily based on lecture.

Lectures should not be deleted from your teaching methods, however. Teaching and learning using lectures can be very appropriate. But, lecturing should not be the only method. Terenzini and Pascarella (1994) have found that teacher-centered activities such as lecture are not "ineffective" but that "the evidence is equally clear that these conventional methods are not as effective as other, far less frequently used methods" (p. 29). Active learning is a general category of teaching methods that can be inserted into almost any class period or can be used to entirely change what happens during a course.

Fink (1999) describes a model of active learning that involves the individual student (the "self") and others having an experience or a dialogue. In other words, a student can have an internal dialogue (dialogue with self) or an external dialogue with others. Reflective thinking is one method of asking students to have an internal dialogue, while a class discussion or a student-to-student discussion is the second type of dialogue. By incorporating dialogue into your classes, you will be enhancing learning. Fink recommends the following:

- Create small groups of students and have them make a decision or answer a focused question periodically,

- Find ways for students to engage in authentic dialogue with people other than fellow class-mates who know something about the subject (on the web, by email, or live),

- Have students keep a journal or build a "learning portfolio" about their own thoughts, learning, feelings, etc. (¶ 8)

These additions to a class period will encourage students to become more active in their learning and will enhance engagement, transfer of knowledge, and student learning.

APPLYING RUBRICS TO ENHANCE LEARNING

"Learning increases, even in its serendipitous aspects, when learners have a sense of what they are setting out to learn (Loacker, Cromwell, & O'Brien, 1986, p. 47). There are many reasons to use explicit rubrics when making assignments and grading them. A rubric gives faculty and students the specific criteria that will be used to grade student work. Rubrics spell out the details and help to ensure that a faculty member is judging all students using the same set of standards and can help students know, very clearly, what the finished work product should contain. And rubrics can be used to create a learning environment for students—it can be the basis for conversation about student learning and performance.

In general, all of us like to know how we are being judged. When writing a grant, it is very important to know how that grant application will be scored. What are the grantors looking for? What elements are most important? What language seems to be used most often by the granting agency (a question very similar to "what will be on test?", by the way). Before going to a job interview, candidates want to know what the employer is looking for and the requirements for the position. Students are no different when wanting to know what an instructor is looking for in a final product. This is where rubrics can come into play. Rubrics can tell a student how they will be judged without having the faculty member feel that a student is only giving the faculty member what he or she "wants to see."

Rubrics are often given to students in the form of a grid. A grid rubric generally contains several (usually between three and five) levels of mastery on the horizontal line and specific outcomes related to the work product on the vertical line. In addition, in each of the corresponding grid spaces is a space for a description of what specific aspects of work the faculty member expects to see in this mastery level, given the specific outcome. When a student submits the work, the faculty member can use a rubric with additional spaces in the commentary area to add specific comments that are geared toward that students' work. (See Figure 4.1)

Figure 4.1
Grid Rubric

	Excellent Work 4	Adequate Work 3	Poor Work 2	Very Poor Work 1	Score
Specific Outcome for This Work Product	Description of what is expected at this level of mastery for this specific outcome.	Description of what is expected at this level of mastery for this specific outcome.	Description of what is expected at this level of mastery for this specific outcome.	Description of what is expected at this level of mastery for this specific outcome.	
Specific Outcome for This Work Product	Description of what is expected at this level of mastery for this specific outcome.	Description of what is expected at this level of mastery for this specific outcome.	Description of what is expected at this level of mastery for this specific outcome.	Description of what is expected at this level of mastery for this specific outcome.	
Specific Outcome for This Work Product	Description of what is expected at this level of mastery for this specific outcome.	Description of what is expected at this level of mastery for this specific outcome.	Description of what is expected at this level of mastery for this specific outcome.	Description of what is expected at this level of mastery for this specific outcome.	
Specific Outcome for This Work Product	Description of what is expected at this level of mastery for this specific outcome.	Description of what is expected at this level of mastery for this specific outcome.	Description of what is expected at this level of mastery for this specific outcome.	Description of what is expected at this level of mastery for this specific outcome.	

Rubrics do not have to be in a grid format. They can also be more text based. The elements are the same, however. They include levels of mastery, descriptions of specific tasks or outcomes, and space for commentary on the student work. The example rubric (figure 4.2) is used for scoring a case study assignment in an educational psychology course. Students were originally given the rubric that contained the elements for "A" work so that students could more clearly see a description of what was expected. The faculty member gave these blank forms to the students and had them complete a rubric on their own work and submit that with the assignment. An interesting byproduct of this rubric example was that students who honestly completed the rubric prior to handing in the assignment tended to revise their case study in more meaningful ways and were able to increase their scores on the case study assignment.

Figure 4.2
Grid Rubric

Case Study Assignment Rubric

"A" Work 4	"D" Work 1
"B" Work 3	"F" Work 0
"C" Work 2	

Analysis of Case Study   Score _____
Comments: _____

_____

Use of Appropriate Theory   Score _____
Comments: _____

_____

Description of the Problem   Score _____
Comments: _____

_____

Appropriate Grammar and Punctuation   Score _____
Comments: _____

_____

As you begin to think about the data that you have for student learning and how you might revise the course, consider thoughtfully how including rubrics could enhance particular assignments and thus student learning. Rubrics are very useful learning tools for students and faculty. Huba and Freed (2000, pp. 169–172) provide six reasons why we should use rubrics to help students learn:

• Rubrics can show students the standards within the discipline.

• Students can better understand the dimensions of quality within a discipline and in overall performance.

- Input from students about what should go into a rubric can encourage students to become actively involved in setting standards for a course.
- Students can also be involved in creating the descriptions of the specific criteria within an assignment.
- Using rubrics can "open the channels of communication between us and our students and among students themselves" (p. 171). Using rubrics in a student peer-review project has many benefits.
- Rubrics can help faculty give better and more meaningful feedback to students about their work.

CONCLUSION

This chapter has focused on the need to rethink the meaning of teaching and learning. Few would argue with the statement that the purpose of a post-secondary education is for students to learn. How they learn and what the faculty member does to facilitate that learning has been the focus of educational research for hundreds of years. How learning occurs and why it occurs in some students and not others is not something that is fully known. Ongoing attention to learning, cognitive science, organic brain functioning, motivational theory, and many others are rich sources of information that can be used by faculty as they teach in higher education.

With the paradigm shifting from teacher-centered to student-centered teaching, there is a means to use available information to enhance student learning. Focusing on what the student needs to learn and how that student learns best is often how faculty begin the paradigm shift within their own teaching philosophies. Rethinking teaching and learning is a simple concept. The point of education is student learning. It is only by focusing on the learning aspect that the teaching part of the equation begins to take on profound meaning.

When using data to spotlight the areas of a course that need to be revised, the role of teaching and learning is critical. Most syllabi have appropriate outcomes, a listing of reasonable assignments, and a current text that is vetted throughout the discipline. But a syllabus is not the same thing as a course: Outcome statements may be appropriate, but without collaboration between a teacher and student and among peers within a class, all that exists is a static document. "As faculty and administrators in higher education, we are entrusted with the job of designing and delivering advanced education. Enhancing learning is the most important task we will ever attempt as professors" (Halpern & Hakel, 2002, p. 7). Regardless of the discipline or the level of the course, understanding the role of teaching in student learning and how to advance that learning is essential.

Chapter Five

Embedding Assessment Activities in Meaningful Ways

The thought of adding "yet another" thing to an already full course can be overwhelming and seemingly impossible. Yet, because you are reading this book, you must have some belief that using data to enhance a course is a good idea. So, how can additional assessment of student learning activities be added to a course? How can more information and activities possibly be included in those short 50 minutes three times a week?

The answer to this is to incorporate meaningful assessment events into the course and to use or modify existing assignments or activities. There are many opportunities to gather information about what students know and don't know and many methods for using that information to enhance a course. Once you begin to look at the course content and existing activities as learning opportunities for students and as a means for you to know what they are learning, the potential for modifying existing class periods will seem infinite (or at least possible).

Davis (1993) states, "in designing or revising a course, faculty are faced with at least three crucial decisions: what to teach, how to teach it, and how to ensure that students are learning what is being taught" (p. 3). This chapter will help you identify what should be taught by creating or revising current teaching goals for a particular course, and it will help you create and then embed learning activities and assignments into your course that will encourage active student learning and provide you with information about what students are learning so that you will be better able to make educational and course-based decisions to enhance student learning.

OUTLINE YOUR TEACHING GOALS

Depending on how long you have been teaching, you may have a teaching portfolio or other collection of information on your teaching. If you already have a list of goals for a particular class, review them carefully to ensure that they are the goals that you still consider to be the most important. If you haven't done this teaching-goal activity in the past, now is a good time! "Goals are ends we work toward, destinations we set out for, results we strive to achieve. But goals are far more than terminal points. They are also reference points that we use to measure our progress and to determine whether we are headed in the right direction" (Angelo & Cross, 1993, p. 13). Teaching goals are important because they help you to more clearly define what you want to happen and can be used to make certain that you and your students are moving toward that point.

There are several ways to think about your teaching goals and learning outcomes for your students. The Angelo and Cross (1993) version of the Teaching Goals Inventory is "a self-assessment of instructional goals" (p. 20). This simple inventory asks you to rate the importance of 52 goals. From this, you can discern where you fall into six clusters of goals that include higher-order thinking skills, basic academic success skills, discipline-specific knowledge and skills, liberal arts and academic values, work and career preparation, and personal development.

There are a variety of other means to look at your teaching goals. A simple online search will probably bring up several tools, some of which are self-scoring on the web for little or no cost. Or, you can write a list of the things that you consider to be most important to you in terms of what you want students to do and learn in a particular course. Asking yourself questions about what you value as a teacher and what you want your students to achieve and to appreciate are all good methods for developing a list of your teaching goals. You can also use the *ideal student* technique to create this list. Ask yourself what the ideal student looks like after taking your course. What things can she or he do? What knowledge can she or he use? What activities have been completed? What values and goals does this ideal student have? (See Chapter 6 for using the ideal student activity to develop student learning outcomes; see Chapter 8 for using the ideal student activity to write a departmental mission statement.)

Developing teaching goals is not a simple task! And, each time you look at your goals, you may want to modify them as you and your teaching may have changed since the last time you focused on the goals. This is a wonderful opportunity to rethink what you want from the perspective of what is possible in your class. Another way to identify teaching goals is to "imagine yourself overhearing a group of graduating seniors who have taken your course and are discussing why it was among the most valuable courses they have ever taken. What would they be saying about the course?" (Davis, 1993, p. 5).

Once your teaching goals are outlined and you have a clear understanding of what these goals are, consider how a person might align your goals with your current syllabus, student work, and assignments. Is the alignment clear? Or, are there some goals and assignments that fit together well and others that don't quite mesh? In some cases, you may find that a goal that you hold to be important doesn't seem to be demonstrated in any assignment or student activity. Or, you may have an assignment that doesn't seem to meet any particular goal or combination of goals. At this point, you will need to carefully review what your current teaching and in-class assignments and activities demonstrate in relation to your goals.

You might consider pairing up with someone in your department or college to get another perspective on your teaching goals. Having a partner in this process can be a benefit to both. Often, the discussion of teaching goals with another person will bring up questions such as:

• Are these goals appropriate for my discipline and teaching style?
• Do I really believe that these goals are the essence of my course?
• Am I missing something that is so obvious that I don't state it in words?
• Are there areas that I haven't included in my teaching goals?

The teaching and learning discussions with colleagues that follow this activity can be a wonderful addition to any course revision or redesign. By asking a colleague to work with you on this, you are creating a "shared vocabulary" (Angelo & Cross, 1993). In addition, you are increasing the likelihood that discussions on teaching and learning will become more explicit and you may increase the departmental interest in using student-learning data to make specific educational decisions.

REVIEW CURRENT TEACHING AND IN-CLASS ACTIVITIES

After creating or revising your list of teaching goals and lining them up with your course activities and events, you will see if (and where) there are gaps in the alignment between what you think you want students to learn and what you are actually asking them to do.

Gather material from the last time you taught the course: syllabus, textbooks, handouts, exams, lecture notes, student evaluations, mid-semester evaluation results, and any other documents relating to the course. Then consider additional aspects of your course:

- What readings are you asking students to do? And, do these readings help students reach a goal?
- What types of homework are you asking from students? What goals do these help you to see in terms of your students' learning?
- What in-class activities are students working on? How do these activities lead students to learning that is important and identified in your teaching goals list?

Go through your syllabus and your course outline day-by-day, listing the events. There are often class activities that you do that aren't identified in your syllabus or in any specific way but could be wonderful tools to find out what students know or don't know. Do you have in-class writing assignments? Do your students work in small groups? Do you have presentations done in class by individual students or a group of students? What types of experiential activities are your students doing? These types of questions may encourage you to look at your course differently. You will see that there are many opportunities to gather information on what students are learning and on how well they are learning the material you want.

In addition, you will more clearly see which of your teaching goals are being met in meaningful ways and which need more support in terms of course assignments and activities. For example, a faculty member in the education department listed critical thinking as a prominent teaching goal. However, when she looked closely at the assignments and activities that she had students do over the semester, there were very few that asked the students to think critically about a particular issue or question. One of these assignments was a paper that students turned in at the end of the semester. The instructor was always discouraged about the lack of critical thinking of her students as demonstrated by that paper. After she tried to align assignments and activities with goals, she realized that she never asked students to be critical thinkers until that last assignment.

This faculty member redesigned her course to include several activities that led up to the final paper and discovered that students could better meet the goal of critical thinking. She didn't change the final paper, but she modified the in-class activities and the ways that students interacted with the reading to better address issues of critical thinking and content. Because she knew what the goals of her course were and was able to look objectively at her course, she was then able to identify an area that needed modification. The changes in her syllabus and assignments made a big difference in what her students were able to demonstrate. The students were better able to think critically about a topic and could demonstrate it in class discussions and writing assignments.

Some of the in-class activities that you are currently using with your students are opportunities for discovering what information students know and these data can be used for assigning grades and for looking at the aggregate knowledge of students. For example, an in-class, graded writing assignment on the topic of environmental damage to a local lake can still be a graded assignment, but it can also be used to look across the class to see areas that are being missed by the majority of students. What don't they seem to understand? What causes are not mentioned by students? The answers to these questions may provide you with information to modify the assignment or the methods used to introduce students to the topic or the assignment. Thus, you can use an assignment to gather data on what students are learning in order to enhance their learning by revising particular aspects of the course. In this manner you can gather data concerning student learning from almost any assignment in the course.

Ungraded assignments are often overlooked in terms of the important information that they can provide you with concerning what students know. But what instructor hasn't listened to a class discussion and known which students understood the material and which ones did not? These more qualitative methods can give rich information to you about how to approach a topic differently or modify an existing assignment. In addition to class discussions, what about in-class writing assignments that are also ungraded? While these are learning tools for students, they're also information about student knowledge for you. The minute paper works very well as an ungraded assignment. (See Chapter 2 for a full description of the minute paper.) Ask students to write and turn their minute papers at the end of class. You can use the information provided in these brief papers to see what students can demonstrate. Based on the information you receive, you might want to start the next class period with a short review of the issue pointing out errors in the overall student responses. You might also consider modifying your lecture notes or in-class activities to highlight areas where students seem to have lower levels of understanding.

Consider Adapting Existing Activities

Adapting existing class activities and assignments and other current activities is an excellent method for increasing student learning and gaining information on what students know. Remember, the goal of gathering data is not to add "yet another" item or task to the long list of student assignments and exams. Rather, the goal is to use the time more effectively to get students actively engaged in the material and to use the resulting information to revise a class or an entire course.

There are several major categories of student work and activities in any particular course. These include:

• Lecture
• Small-group discussion
• Full-class discussion
• Papers
• Exams
• Oral presentations
• Experiential activities
• Out-of-class assignments (homework, projects)
• Reading material (ideally prior to class, but often done prior to exams)
• Course evaluations

Over the course of a semester, you probably are already using several of these to provide students with information and to assess what students know. The student work that is submitted is often submitted for a grade. But consider how some of these types of student work might be used to gather information about what students know so that you can enhance a course in progress or revise it for the next time it is taught.

Lecture

"Lecturing is not simply a matter of standing in front of a class and reciting what you know" (Davis, 1993, p. 111). To lecture well, an instructor must hold the attention of his or her students and engage them in thinking about the material presented. There are many things that go into the creation of a good lecture. Some of these are fundamental: good content, up-to-date information, relevant examples. Other aspects to a good lecture include eye contact, facial expressions, and a loud enough voice to be heard throughout the classroom—things that can be learned and easily added. While active learning, small-group work, and class discussions are pedagogical methods that are often praised as being "better" than lectures, this isn't always true. Lectures have been and continue to be a time-honored approach to transmitting a large amount of information to students. Many faculty were taught by listening to lectures and they tend to teach in that way.

Lectures can be a good way to teach. But the problems with lectures have to do with the student responses to them. Next time you are lecturing to a class, look around at the students. Are they listening to what you are saying? Are they making eye contact with you? Are they reading the newspaper or checking their email? Another method to see how students are responding to your lecture is to ask to look at their notes at the end of class. Is there a lot of doodling? Are the notes logical and do they capture the main points? By looking at the student responses to lecture, you can gather some very useful information about how much they seem to be paying attention.

Another technique that you can add to a lecture is to intersperse discussion or thought questions throughout the lecture. Many faculty ask questions during lecture, but they don't often expect (or give time for) students to answer. A classic example of this is an extremely accurate scene from the movie *Ferris Bueller's Day Off* (Hughes & Jacobson,1986). The economics teacher, played by Ben Stein, stands in front of an obviously and extremely bored class and says:

> In 1930, the Republican-controlled House of Representatives, in an effort to alleviate the effects of the . . . Anyone? Anyone? . . . the Great Depression, passed the . . . Anyone? Anyone? The tariff bill? The Hawley-Smoot Tariff Act? Which, anyone? Raised or lowered? . . . raised tariffs, in an effort to collect more revenue for the federal government. Did it work? Anyone? Anyone know the effects? It did not work, and the United States sank deeper into the Great Depression.

In this scene there is no time between the asking of the question and the teacher answering the question. Unfortunately, this occurs in many classrooms every day. Many faculty do not wait for a long enough time after asking a question, so students don't have time to respond (or even think about a response) before the question is answered for them by the faculty member. Thus, the faculty member learns that students don't "know" the answer and students learn that they don't have to answer because the questions aren't designed to elicit a response from them.

The concept of *wait time* was defined by Rowe in 1972 and her research shows that the average wait time (the time between the end of the question and the start of an answer) was about 1.5 seconds in elementary classrooms. By increasing the amount of wait to 3 seconds, students' responses were more correct in their answers, answers were more complex and complete, and the number of "I don't know" answers was lessened. In the college classroom, wait time is also very important. Asking questions to which you want an answer or response from students is an important part of the learning process. In order for this to work, you must give students time to think about the answer before responding. Some faculty feel that this "pregnant pause" in the middle of class is difficult, but they must resist the urge to fill the silence with sound (teacher-talking sound). Give students the chance to think about your question, perhaps even a few minutes to jot down thoughts about it, and then give them time to answer it in class and stay with the question until it is complete. By having students think about the answer (even if only one responds), you are asking them to be active in their learning and this alone can increase retention of material and engagement in the course.

Small-Group Discussion and Full-Class Discussion

Having students talk about an issue in a small group or as a class during class time has several advantages. It allows each student more time to talk about an issue and to hear comments and thoughts from other students in the group. In a small-group discussion, these comments and thoughts tend to be longer and more complex than those that are given within an entire class discussion where time for any one student's comments is limited.

According to McKeachie (1986), discussion is most appropriate when a faculty member wants to:

- Help students learn to think in terms of the subject matter by giving them practice in thinking.

- Help students learn to evaluative the logic of, and evidence for, their own and others' positions.

- Give students opportunities to formulate applications of principles.

- Help students become aware of and formulate problems using information gained from readings or lectures.

- Use the resources of members of the group.

- Gain acceptance for information or theories counter to folklore or previous beliefs of students.

- Develop motivation for further learning.

- Get prompt feedback on how well objectives are being attained. (p. 27)

However, having discussions in class is difficult when faculty see them as taking time away from a lecture. A faculty member might say, "if the students are talking about the issue, some might be wrong, others might take a long time to get the point. Wouldn't it be faster and easier to have a lecture on the topic?" The logic in this statement is obvious. It is more "efficient" to lecture in terms of telling students information. However, students don't always learn something just because they hear it or write it in their notes. Students often gain new information when they are able to think and talk about the issue, developing arguments or thinking critically about the issue. Discussions have a place in classroom time—they may not be the best means of telling students information, but they are an effective method for engaging students in the topic at hand.

Full-class discussions can sometimes be difficult to get started; asking a question is usually the best strategy. By starting from a common experience (the lecture, readings, a video, or a speaker), students have a place from which to begin. Questions such as "what issues were outlined in the readings?" might be too big of an opening question, but it can be honed down to something that is more specific like "which issue seemed to be the most important?" Depending on how comfortable students are with participating in a discussion, you can vary the type of question used to begin. As students respond, move around the room (away from the speaker). This will make the speaker talk louder because she or he is trying to have you hear the comment. Ask students to respond to a comment or to consider other possibilities. Full-class discussions can be as long or short as you desire. Usually, the more complex the question or issue, the longer the discussion should be. When students are not able to outline the issues or points that you would like them to know, this gives you information about their level of knowledge. Perhaps, based on what you hear from students during the discussion, you decide that they need more background information. In this case, you could send them information via email, hand out additional information in the next class period, or choose to explain information that was already given. In any case, knowing what students know is a valuable tool when revising a single class period or an entire course.

If students are involved in small-group discussions, the faculty member can move throughout the classroom to listen to what students are saying. This enables the faculty member to pick up on misconceptions or errors that are being discussed. And, when this happens, the discussions can be stopped and a clarification or correction can be made to the entire class. This type of qualitative data (students are discussing the use of negative reinforcement as if it were punishment) can be used to make the correction and add to information that students receive during the next time the course is taught. In addition, as the faculty member is listening in on discussions, students will tend to stay "on topic" as they see their instructor move closer. Finally, asking students to report out at the end of the discussion in some way can bring closure to the discussion. Depending on the size of the class, you may want to hear from each group, or perhaps you could listen to specific comments from only a few. Michaelson, Knight, and Fink (2002) outline an effective technique for using team-based learning. In this type of small-group discussion, teams of students go through specific structured activities in which the team teaches, learns, and discusses the concepts in class.

Papers and Exams

Almost every college-level course has graded exams and paper assignments. These traditional methods for assessing individual student learning can also be used as data to determine areas of a course that need revising. Nothing is quite as frustrating as reading a set of papers on a topic that was discussed, lectured on, and discussed some more, yet clearly indicates that the students do not have an in-depth understanding of the issue on which the paper or essay question was written. While this is frustrating, it can also be a springboard to ask questions like "why did so many students miss the main point?" or "how could this information be presented differently so that more students might better understand the issue?"

Asking these kinds of questions can change your perspective in terms of how to use this information. When answering a question like "why did so many students miss the point?" you can look across student work rather than looking (with frustration) at an individual student who "should have known." In some cases, the problem might be that students didn't completely understand the assignment and so their work isn't representative of their knowledge. In this case, you could expect to see student knowledge of the issues or topics appear in other assignments or class discussions. It might also be, however, that students do not know the information that you want them to know. If the content or skill knowledge appears to be lacking in many other areas, the issue may be that students are not learning the material. This leads to additional questions such as "how are students supposed to get the material?" and "are there other ways to address these topics in and out of class so that students have additional opportunities to learn?" By following through with these questions, you can begin to see where a course could be modified in sequencing and in class activities. With the data provided by exams or papers, you can find where there are gaps in their aggregate knowledge and attempt to fill those gaps.

Oral Presentations

Hearing students present information individually or in a group format can be insightful! In order to present information well, it is essential that the student have more than a mere comprehension of the material. The student must have in-depth knowledge of a topic and understand connections within that topic to other areas of the course. Sitting through a presentation when it is clear that the student does not have this information can be painful. Oral presentations are another category that can serve as both a learning tool for students (they gain information as they prepare for their presentation plus they learn communication and critical thinking skills) and as a means to determine how much a student knows (assigning a grade or looking for knowledge gaps).

Oral presentations can be designed to fill an entire class period with a single student or group of students assigned to teach the topic to the class, or they can be short, focusing on a particular area within the main topic for that class period. Often, faculty assign oral presentations to include some written document (e.g., PowerPoint slides, outline, handouts, or a mini-paper) that go along with the oral presentation or add information. Designing the assignment so that students can successfully learn the material and competently teach it to the class is crucial since having to "re-teach" it because of errors can be a costly use of time and can cause confusion among the students. Students should clearly know what the assignment is, what they should cover, and what supplemental materials they will need. Some faculty require that students submit their written documents prior to the oral presentation so that areas of misunderstanding can be corrected before the presentation. This is a good idea and also ensures that the student or group is prepared for the time of the oral presentation.

A faculty member in communications has students prepare several 15-minute presentations throughout the semester. Each time, the student is evaluated on several areas including content, presentation style, and multimedia support. The student presentation is scored by the instructor and by members of the class. The class members must make appropriate evaluative comments regarding the presentation that tie in with the material of the course. This requires that the oral presentation be a tool for the student giving the presentation and for fellow students who are watching the presentation. The evaluations all go to the faculty member who then shares them with the individual student presenter. By keeping copies of students' and his own evaluations, the faculty member can later look back and see areas that show student improvement and knowledge and areas that still need to be addressed for the individual student and as a class. These documents become a rich source of data to revise a course. Based on previous semesters, the faculty member included additional short presentations to address specific issues of eye contact and voice as these seemed to be areas that did not improve for a majority of students over the course of the semester.

Experiential Activities

Having students experience learning activities that are very close to "real life" is often called experiential learning. These activities can include simulations in class, service-learning opportunities, and other events in which students are learning by doing. These kinds of learning opportunities can and should be embedded in the class-room, because they stimulate learning by causing students to become active participants in the content and in the construction of their own learning.

There are many different types of experiential learning that you can offer your students. Many textbooks outline these types of activities in an instructor manual.

These can be very useful and can often be easily modified for your course size and specific needs. Some experiential learning activities are complex and may take an entire class period or more. One example of this is an activity that an education instructor used. This experiential learning event took three class periods and involved student preparation and small-group work between class periods. Students were placed into groups and asked to design a community. They had to give it a name, draw it out, and describe its inhabitants, history, and culture. Each group started with a set of relatively arbitrary rules that had to be integrated into the culture (eye contact in one group showing respect, no eye contact in another, for example). Students had time in class to physically draw out their community and bond with the team. Then, in the second class period, some students were moved from each team so that there were new groups of students that were mixed together. The groups were given a task, but they had to keep their cultural norms as set during the first class period. During the third class period students discussed what it was like to do the task with people from another culture. They talked about how it felt to be in the minority and how it felt to have minority members join their group. The students indicated that the experiential activity was very meaningful and taught them a great deal about diversity and multiculturalism—student responses actually showed that students who had participated in the experiential simulation were better able to apply what they had learned in other diversity-related cases.

It is important to follow up on these activities to ensure that students are actually learning what you want them to learn. Some experiential learning can just be seen as fun by students and not produce the types of learning that are expected. By checking to see how students respond and what they are learning, you can make certain that students are meeting the outcomes that you have set for them.

These types of experiential activities can be powerful learning opportunities for students. They require significant up-front preparation on the part of the faculty member, but they can be very worthwhile in the amount of student learning that they can produce.

Out-of-Class Activities

You can increase the amount of time that students are involved with the content by having students prepare for class beforehand and respond to what they learned in class afterward. Their academic engagement with your class will increase by having specific out-of-class learning opportunities. These may be homework assignments, small-group work that is done outside of normal class time, or preparation of a paper or project. In any case, these can present many sources of data for you to use to see how students are learning. For example, after homework has been submitted and graded for individual work, look back at the homework to see if there are areas where students seem to be making errors. If so, consider modifying your teaching before this homework assignment so that students get additional information or practice so that they can better demonstrate their knowledge on that homework assignment. This type of assessment can be done with all learning activities, but the out-of-class activities provide students with additional time to be engaged with the material and, thus, provide you with substantial data on how well they understand the material.

Course Evaluations

While course evaluations are used for many things in higher education, their primary purpose should be course enhancement. The information that students give regarding their perceptions of teaching should be taken into consideration. However, because they are a sample of student responses taken at the end of the semester, they should not be the only data that is used to revise a course. Taking multiple measures of student reports about teaching is crucial. So, asking questions about how much correlation there is between a mid-semester versus an end-of-semester evaluation can give a better viewpoint than only looking at end-of semester evaluations.

Course evaluations do give information, but the information that they give is not usually data on student learning. Rather, it is on how students perceive the course, their feelings regarding the instructor and the course, and their opinions on what they believe should have occurred in the course. Ensuring that your course is revised using data about student learning rather than student self-report is important and relying only on course evaluations may give a skewed view of student learning in the course.

CREATE NEW METHODS TO ASSESS STUDENT LEARNING

As you look through the activities that you are currently using to measure student learning, and you look through this book or other information to find new methods, consider the following as you think about what to add to your course:

- Does this activity or method feel somewhat comfortable to me?
- Will this work given the size of my class?

• Does this fit into my philosophy of teaching?
• Will this event help students become more engaged in the material and bring them closer to meeting the objectives for the course?

If you can respond "yes" to several of these, then the activity you are thinking of adding may be a very good fit for your course. While you may not feel completely comfortable with a new activity, you will probably find that you become more comfortable with it as you use it and as you see students respond to it. It is not always easy to add something new—it may take you and your students outside your comfort zone, but it may be the best thing that you ever did for your course.

You may find that nothing that you see actually meets the needs of you or your students. In this case, you may need to create or modify an existing assessment activity or teaching method to meet your needs. Consider the questions listed here as you create the new activity, focusing particularly on whether this change will help students become more engaged in the material and bring them closer to meeting the objectives for the course. This is the crucial question and is essential to enhance student learning and give you the type of data that you need to redesign your course.

THE IMPORTANCE OF EMBEDDING ACTIVITIES

The amount of time that students have for studying and class preparation seems to be decreasing every semester. Students have additional work-related activities, cocurricular responsibilities, and what seems like an ever-decreasing amount of time for study. In addition, faculty time is tight. Between research, committee work and other service, family responsibilities, and advising and mentoring, there is little time left to put into course redesign. But, by embedding activities into the course, using activities that you already have in place or replacing an old activity with a more meaningful one, you can enhance student learning while gathering classroom assessment information from your students.

As you redesign your course or as you think about what data you need to make important, meaningful decisions about an existing course, think about what types of data you already have. Students are probably already submitting homework, papers, and completing exams. These can all be used as sources of data and should not be overlooked. You also already have end-of-semester student responses and gathering some at mid-semester can be done with a minimum investment of class time. But the results can be worth the time! By knowing what students are learning and how they respond to the course, you can make curricular decisions that are based on data and you will know what works and what doesn't. This means that your time in class and outside of class will be used in the best possible way. And, your students' learning will be a guide to enhancing their learning even more.

Chapter Six

Planning The Course

*I*n order to teach a course successfully, there must be a certain amount of preparation put into each class session, but also prior to the start of the course. The design and planning of a course can be as little as blowing the dust off of notes from last semester, changing the dates in the syllabus, and reordering the textbook, or it can be as involved as completely redesigning the course including student outcomes, order of topics, and pedagogical approach to class. This chapter focuses on the latter, but any single aspect can be applied without necessarily using the entire course revision process. The concept to keep in mind is that the outcome should be something that will get students to learn what they need to learn, provide the opportunities for engagement and interaction with the material, measure student learning to appropriately assign grades, and meet your needs as a teacher. Most would agree that getting students to learn and interact with material is crucial, but keeping the instructor motivated and excited to teach is also important.

STUDENT LEARNING OUTCOMES AND OTHER DATA SOURCES

Creating appropriate student learning outcomes or goals for your specific course is an important first step. Clearly, you would expect different skills and knowledge from an introductory course than you would a senior-level course. What do you want students to know at the end of the semester? What skills should they have? What experiences should they be able to report on? A slightly truncated version of the ideal student activity can be used at the course level. When a student completes your course, what, ideally, does that student know? What skills do you want this student to be able to perform? What theoretical perspectives should this ideal student be able to describe and/or apply?

As part of the process of listing student learning outcomes, consider also the expectations that you have of students entering the course. Are there prerequisite skills or courses that they should have? Do you expect students to already be familiar with elements of the subject matter? The expected prior knowledge or experiences of your students will give you a better perspective on what you want students to bring into the course with them. This can then become part of the syllabus or course description. Not all students will enter your course with all of the skills or knowledge that you would like, but before you build or redesign your course, knowing what information you expect them to have at the beginning is important as it will help you to frame the course.

These student learning goals should be listed in the syllabus so that all participants in the course know what is expected of them. Students know what they are expected to learn and it helps to focus the creation of the teaching and learning activities more clearly. For example, your course probably has specific content goals that students need as part of the requirements for a major or for general education. In addition to these content-based objectives, what other goals do you have for your students? Do you want to include student learning outcomes related to critical thinking? Analysis of problems? Synthesis of ideas and concepts? Some of these goals are broad and may not be demonstrated by a single assignment or activity. Critical thinking is something, for example, that takes a great deal of practice and time. For most students, growth in critical thinking is more important than "completing" something.

As you are considering the outcomes that you want students to have as they complete your course, you will likely see issues that are part of your teaching philosophy. In other words, your goals will probably reflect your beliefs about what a "teacher" should be and what a "student" should be. Using the example of critical thinking again, it is likely that a faculty member who believes that part of the purpose of the course is to have students think critically about course-related topics will have assignments and activities that ask students to think critically. Sometimes, however, there is a disconnect between what the faculty member believes and what occurs in the course. By taking the time to consider your teaching philosophy and aligning your philosophy with the course outcomes and the course outline/activities, you will ensure that what you believe to be important for students to learn is, in fact, what they focus on inside and outside of the class.

Other Data Sources

Besides using student learning information from previous semesters, you should also consider how your course is integrated into the major or department. Many departments are now using program review or departmental assessment data to demonstrate student learning. This information can also be used to look at an individual course, provided that the department-level student outcomes are part of what is taught in the specific course you are working on.

Program-review data likely contains information about what students are learning, how they perceive their academic experiences within the department, and how the department is benchmarked against other institutions or departments. Regardless of the type of information that is included, you can probably use aspects of it to inform the decisions you are making about your course. For example, a faculty member in English was revising a poetry course. The responses from previous students indicated that while they learned quite a bit about writing poetry and completed several types of poems, they did not enjoy the course. Qualitative comments on student evaluations demonstrated that students were bored during class and felt that they weren't allowed to be creative and write what they wanted to write. The faculty member looked at data from the departmental program review and found similar aggregate attitudes from students. In addition, she noted that senior-level students had lower instances of responding that there were not enough opportunities to be creative in writing. As she looked at the different formats that the upper-level courses used, she noticed that these courses did have more opportunities for writing. She thought about the process, worked with the campus teaching center, and made some data-based decisions about what she could do to revise her course. She felt that the objectives of the course should remain focused on learning to write using different forms of poetry. She felt that students who didn't enjoy writing these different forms might still feel constrained, but that it was important to teach these formats. However, she added a larger portfolio project to her class and required students to make reflective responses to the work that they were doing on a regular basis. The final portfolio that students submitted in that class became a large project with poems, reflections on the poems from the readings and original works by the student, and an additional final poem that could be written in any format. This final poem had to include an analysis of the form used. In addition, the faculty member added group time in class so that students could read and respond to each other's work using the analysis technique taught in class. Based on mid-semester and end-of-semester feedback, students taking the revised course felt that they were applying much more what they had learned. Their satisfaction ratings for the course improved significantly.

Another source of data is student comments and satisfaction ratings from end-of-semester course evaluations. As with any self-report survey, there are several variables that impact course evaluation results that are not directly related to teaching effectiveness (Baldwin & Blattner, 2003). These factors include time of day of the class, level of the class, and class size. Even with the potential bias contained within course evaluations, they can still be used as information for course revision. An informal trend analysis using student comments or other issues can be useful. Take out several past student evaluations for the course you are interested in revising. Reread the student comments and look at the overall quantitative scores. Are there issues that seem to repeat from semester to semester? These are the areas to focus on—both the positive trends (students love the class discussions) and any low-scored areas (students respond that the class is unorganized). The areas that students seem to report that they enjoy or learn from are areas to consider maintaining or enhancing in the course. Those areas that seem to indicate problems or student dissatisfaction should be looked at to determine if changes are appropriate.

The data from student evaluations should align with other data sources that are direct measures of student learning. Making a change to take out an assignment that students don't like, yet seem to learn a lot from is probably not something that should be done; however, if the assignment doesn't seem to increase student learning and the students report dissatisfaction, then making a change to that assignment is rational. Look for alignment among course objectives, student learning, and student satisfaction. Unfortunately, you won't always see the alignment. Sometimes students will report a dislike for a particular part of the course, but it is an area that is important in terms of outcomes. Clearly, that content is something that must stay in the course; however, you might consider different ways to approach the content. Moving from a lecture to a team-learning approach could increase student learning and student satisfaction.

Course evaluations are a source of data about teaching—but they are based on student perceptions and, thus, should be used along with other data sources to make the best decisions about your course that will lead to increased student learning. Student satisfaction is often a good thing, but it should never become more important than student learning.

TEACHING AND LEARNING ACTIVITIES

After considering outcomes and data, it is time to make specific decisions about which teaching and learning activities and assignments will be kept in the course, which will be modified, and which will be deleted. In addition, making choices about the new additions to a course must be considered as well. Looking back over the outcomes for the course, some of the first decisions to make concern removing those "policies and practices that are at odds with what an instructor believes about students and learning" (Weimer, 1990, p. 38). Weimer adds that "the choice of what to change need not always become the negative perspective. The choice may be to change by doing more of some aspect of teaching that does sit well with an instructor's philosophy or with those who experience its effects" (p. 39).

You know what you want students to know or be able to do by the end of the course; this information is described in the outcomes you have outlined. Now you must consider how you will know when the students have reached an outcome. What will a student need to do in order to indicate that she or he knows the information? The answers to this question will help you consider the types of assignments (usually graded assignments, but they don't necessarily have to be) that you should be having students complete. For example, if one of your outcomes is that students will be able to properly identify a type of research methodology to use, what should they be able to do? Will a response on a multiple choice test be enough to demonstrate this knowledge? Or, do you need students to respond in a paper? Or, in a class presentation? Or, do you want students to design a research study and carry it out? These are decisions that you should be making before you start to create the day-to-day grading aspect of your course. If you do want students to create a research design and then carry out the research, you will need to devote additional time to this activity versus a response on an essay test. You may also want to break down the project into specific parts that students complete over the course of the semester. By making decisions about what students need to be able to demonstrate in order to assure you that they have met the objective, you will be redesigning the assignments and activities that they will need to do to be prepared.

Many faculty find it useful to create a matrix that lists the course outcomes on one axis and the course assignments on the other. A lack of activities and/or assignments in relationship to the outcomes indicates a need for closer inspection of the assignments. Are there embedded activities (see chapter 5) that you want to include? Are there specific outcomes that are not fully met by many students and might need additional time in class? Could a large project with several parts actually meet more than one objective?

As you consider assignments and course activities, make sure that these all fit into your objectives for the course. Just because an activity is interesting or different doesn't necessarily mean that it helps you to meet student learning needs in your class. In addition, ensure that many of the activities require students to become active learners. Active learning occurs when students are actually doing activities and they are also thinking about the activities in which they are involved (Bonwell & Eison, 1991). In addition to being actively and behaviorally involved, having students think about the information is crucial. How are students reflecting on what they know? Are you asking them to think about the material? Are they able to relate the new information from this course to other information that they already have? Thinking

about new information in a variety of ways helps increase
student learning; this can be done by asking students to
think of examples or events that are specific to information
from the course.

Once you have a workable draft of a matrix indicating
that your outcomes are being addressed by assignments
and class activities, look at resources that you will use for
student learning. Ask questions such as, "what information
will students need to have in order to successfully complete
the assignments?" and "where should this information
come from?" You will need to consider aspects of the
resources such as:

• Is the existing textbook the one that you still want to
  use? Does it meet your needs?
• Are there additional readings? Lab reports? Reprints?
• Besides text-based resources, consider video information.
  Are there film clips? News broadcasts?
• What about guest speakers?
• Are there specific community or campus-wide events
  that might give students additional information or a
  different perspective on a topic related to your course?

There are a variety of sources of material for your
course. Limiting the resources can be useful, because it
allows students to focus more closely on the things that
you want them to learn. However, you might consider
having students work on finding some of these resources
during the semester. In the case of student research on a
particular topic, part of the learning process may be the
search for information, rather than the end product.
Consider having students take some responsibility for
finding appropriate resources either through library
research or current events. They can share this information
with the class and it can become part of the course.

GRADING POLICIES AND PROCESSES

There are a couple of questions that come up every semester that faculty have come to expect and dislike: "Will this be on the test?" and "How many points do I get for ____?" But these questions deal with aspects of grading and grading polices for a particular course. There are, of course, many different ways to develop a grading system. Some faculty are very "strict" about assignments and grades, while others are more lenient. Some maintain the same grading "personality" all semester, others modify it once they get to know the students in a particular course. In addition, the level and maturity of the students in the class can impact grading philosophies and policies. Freshmen taking an introductory course might encounter a stricter policy than when taking a more advanced course later on with the same faculty member.

Regardless of the particular philosophy, grading student work should be fair, equitable, consistent, timely, and faculty should be able to defend the grade given to a student. Students should perceive (and that perception should be accurate) that they are being assigned a grade that is based on the quality of their work, its timeliness (when appropriate), and not on irrelevant variables. If students perceive that grading is not fair (even if it is), there will be problems that seep into the course. Grading should never come as a surprise. Students should know what they are to do, what support is available to them, and how their work will be graded. Using specific and explicit rubrics can help, but faculty should work diligently to ensure that students know what to expect and when to expect it. While you may choose to have surprise graded events such as pop quizzes, students still need to know that these events could happen. Major assignments should be scheduled at the beginning of the semester so that students at least have the opportunity to schedule in appropriate time for the work.

There are several ways to look at the various types of philosophies that faculty hold with regard to grading. In the handbook *Instruction at FSU: A Guide to Teaching and Learning Practices* (Instructional Development Services, 2002), several philosophies of grading are outlined:

> *Philosophy #1* — Grades are indicators of relative knowledge and skill; that is, a student's performance can and should be compared to the performance of other students in that course. The standard to be used for the grade is the average score of the class on a test, paper, or project.

> *Philosophy #2* — Grades are based on preset expectations or criteria. In theory, every student in the course could get an A if each of them met the preset expectations. The grades are usually expressed as the percentage of success achieved.

> *Philosophy #3* — Students come into the course with an A, and it is theirs to lose through poor performance or absence, late papers, etc. With this philosophy the teacher takes away points, rather than adding them.

> *Philosophy #4* — Grades are subjective assessments of how a student is performing according to his or her potential. Students who plan to major in a subject should be graded harder than a student just taking a course out of general interest. Therefore, the standard set

depends upon student variables and shouldn't be set in stone. (p. 13.1)

Regardless of your specific philosophy of grading, make sure that it is communicated clearly to students and is in line with the expectations of your department or college. And, if changes need to be made in either your philosophy or the specific grading polices, make certain that students know this as soon as possible and they are not put at a disadvantage by the change.

Rubrics

Rubrics outline the criteria that will be used to grade a particular assignment. Some rubrics are very formal, while others are not. Often faculty who don't use formal text-based rubrics still use a rubric. They know what they are looking for in a response to an essay question or a paper. A rubric is "an assessment tool that lists the criteria for a piece of work....and articulates gradations of quality for each criterion" (Andrade, 2005, p. 27). There are several benefits to using formal, written rubrics. The first is that when grading student work you know that you are assigning points based on the same criteria for each student work product that you evaluate. The second benefit of rubrics is that when handed out to students beforehand, the student knows how she or he will be graded and can make adjustments to the quality or format of work accordingly. Some faculty actually ask students to rate their own work on the rubric before submitting it. This can lead to more complete and higher quality work in many cases.

Andrade (2005) claims, "instructional rubrics help me clarify my expectations and focus my instruction" (p. 27). As you create a rubric, you are envisioning the end product that you wish for students to submit. This can lead to a better explanation to students about the assignment and how it will be graded. The creation of rubrics can be a simple process with a few general steps.

1) List the criteria that are necessary for an exemplary final product. This list of criteria might involve basic elements such as format, spelling, and professionalism, but will also contain specific aspects of the content. For example, in a psychology course the final research paper must appropriately outline the methodology used.

2) Describe the levels of quality for each of the criterion. These may correspond to A, B, or C work or you might want to be more qualitative and describe it as "excellent," "average," and "poor." Consider how many levels you wish to outline. Three to five levels of quality are often used, but you can have as many as you would like. Keep in mind, however, that the more levels of quality the more fine the distinction between each.

3) Write the draft of the rubric. Some rubrics are handed out in the form of a table or matrix while some are text-based and more narrative. There is no "right" way to do this. However, it might be helpful to you to look at rubrics that colleagues have used.

4) Revise the draft of the rubric as needed.

Rubrics can be very useful as they can help facilitate "a shared understanding of the expected performance between students and teachers. The rubrics also make it easier and less time consuming for the teacher to grade the assignment because of clearly delineated expectations" (Hall & Salmon, 2003, p. 10–11).

Norm-Referenced versus Criterion-Referenced Grading

The decision regarding how to judge a student's work is a very important one. Do you want to grade each student based on the work of other students in the class (norm-referenced) or do you want to measure each student's work against a set of established criteria (criterion-referenced)?

With norm-referenced grading you will be comparing the work of one student against others. This will cause a spread in the grade distribution and cause it to have a more bell-shaped, normal curve. This can be useful if there is only a certain percentage of students who can continue on to the next level in the major. If you want to "weed out" the bottom 25 % of students in the class, for example, you might choose to use norm-referenced grading. Norm-referenced grading has several side effects that are directly related to student learning, however. One is that students are competing against each other: If Student A can cause another one to do badly, Student A will do better regardless of the actual amount of learning done by Student A. McKeachie (1986) says that "grading on a curve stacks the cards against cooperative learning, because helping classmates may lower one's own grade" (p. 105).

Criterion-referenced grading, on the other hand, compares the work of individual students against set criteria. All students could do well, or all students could fail. One student's score is not dependent on the scores of other students in the course. This type of grading can encourage collaboration and is the most commonly used method for grading in most college and university courses. "The principle underlying criterion-referenced grading is that a student's grade reflects his or her level of achievement, independent of how other students in the class have performed" (Davis, 1993, p. 289).

Some faculty also believe that the level of individual student improvement should be taken into consideration when assigning grades. The problem with implementing this system is that students who get the same final grade in the course may not have reached the same level of performance or knowledge. A student with no knowledge of the subject at the beginning of the class may learn a lot by the end, but not as much as a student who came in with information on the subject matter. In addition, "grading on the basis of improvement also makes it difficult for students [and others] to interpret what their grades mean: does a B mean that their work is above average or that their improvement is above average?" (Davis, 1993, p. 290).

Attendance Grading

The decision to use attendance as part of the grading scale is based on several factors. The first is departmental and university policy. If the policy clearly states that attendance is to be used as a factor in the final grade, it is something that should be included. Another factor is the teaching philosophy of the individual faculty member. Some faculty feel that attendance is important and the way to get students to attend class is to reward them with points (or penalize them by removing points). Other faculty choose not to take attendance because they believe that students should take responsibility for their learning and that the choice to attend class is one that the student should make, accepting the consequences for missing information or material.

In this case, there is no one "right" answer. But, if there is no departmental or university policy, deciding whether to take and use attendance is an important one. Students want to know what goes into the final grade. Therefore, this is a policy that should be outlined in the syllabus and clearly described so that students know what will cause them to gain or lose points. Students should also be told what the consequences are for missing class. How many points do they lose? Can they make up the missed work? Are there differences in consequences if the absence was due to illness or a university-sanctioned event? By responding to these issues in the syllabus and early in the semester, students will know your expectations and they can plan their behavior accordingly.

Grading Strategies and Practices

According to Davis (1993), there are several basic strategies that will encourage student learning and may limit their dissatisfaction or frustration with the grading aspect of the course:

- Grade on the basis of students' mastery of knowledge and skills,

- Avoid grading systems that put students in competition with their classmates and limit the number of high grades,

- Try not to overemphasize grades,

- Keep students informed of their progress throughout the term,

- Clearly state grading procedures in your course syllabus and go over the information in class,

- Set policies on late work,

- Avoid modifying your grading policies during the term,

- Provide enough opportunities for students to show you what they know. (pp. 283–284)

By carefully outlining what is expected of students and what consequences students can expect for their work, students can focus on what they are learning. It is a very frustrating experience to spend time with a student who wants a few more points on an assignment, when it is clear that the student hasn't really learned the material to the appropriate level. Faculty usually want students to think about what they are learning rather than to be focused on only learning something if it is going to be on the test. By helping students understand the grading system, it becomes a structure or a scaffold that is a supporting influence on the course, but is not the focus of the course.

Students are often "over pointed" in classes. They may have been taught to expect that all things that they do will receive points or grades. Therefore, why write a reflection paper if it isn't going to be graded? When the focus is on the points and the grade rather than on the learning, the student and the instructor lose the opportunity to experience the intrinsic joy of learning something. By creating a grading system that students perceive as fair and appropriate, faculty can help to shift the focus to the learning activities and the ideal of lifelong learning.

Enjoyment of Teaching

While much of the information in this book and in other resources on course revision focuses on the centrality of student learning, it is also important that teaching the course is (most often) enjoyable and stimulating for the faculty member. You have probably had wonderful experiences when you left class feeling excited and energized by the student discussions or questions that came up during class. While this may not happen in every class period, it is an important part of the course to keep in mind.

Most faculty did not choose to go into university employment because they loved teaching. Most love the subject matter that they are involved with and teaching that content to interested students can be a stimulating and revitalizing part of the job. Most faculty have some level of passion for their discipline and working with students who share that interest is an enriching experience for both. But not all students share the passion for the subject matter. Some students take a course because they are required to and these students may not show intrinsic motivation to prepare for and participate in class. How, then, can teaching an introductory course, for example, be enjoyable and enriching to the faculty member when the students are not majors and might not even want to be in class?

Part of the reason to revise a course is to enhance student learning. Part of the reason may also be to add elements to the course that will make it a more enriching experience for students. Adding "significant learning experiences" to your course can encourage students to become more involved, to learn more, and to want to be better prepared for class. Fink's (2003) Taxonomy of Significant Learning contains six areas that can interact with each other to create a synergy that makes the whole greater than the sum of the parts. These elements of the taxonomy are:

- Foundational knowledge that is part of the content of the course
- Application of the content to problems, cases, or situations
- Integration among ideas, subject matter, people, etc.
- The human dimension that requires students to learn more about themselves and interactions with others
- Caring about the issues, feelings, or values
- Learning how to learn

As a faculty member, if you can create a situation where students must do more than one of the above, students will probably have a more significant learning experience because of the interactive and synergistic aspect of the elements of the taxonomy. For example, in a social work class, the faculty member wanted students to learn the process of investigating a case that would allow for admission of certain facts into court. Students were assigned readings that outlined the steps required, the basis for collecting evidence, and how to interview appropriately. Thus, they had foundational knowledge. Rather than stop there, the faculty member added another dimension. He asked them to apply the knowledge that they acquired to a particular case study. Rather than give them the entire case study, he gave them part of it. This part was the information that usually comes in when a report has been made to a social services agency. It was a child abuse case, and the students were presented with the initial report from the hospital. Students, in small groups, now had to apply what they knew about the investigation process to determine the information they needed and the questions that they wanted answered. As each group reported out with their requests for information, it was given to them. Each step required that students work together to apply the information to the case. Using application and foundational knowledge, this faculty member encouraged student discussion and questions. Students began to care about the "child" in the case. They began to integrate the information from this course with another prerequisite course. In short, this class period became a significant learning experience for the students. The faculty member did not give them the "correct" answer, he just facilitated and responded to their questions.

The faculty member in this example enjoyed teaching that course. He expressed feelings of joy at seeing students really care about the subject matter and the issues. Going back into that classroom was something that he looked forward to. While not all class periods will be as meaningful as this one, it is important to consider faculty interest. There are several ways to do this. Have a particular "bright spot" in the class that you are looking forward to. Students don't need to know what it is (if it comes in the beginning of the class, they might think it all downhill from there!). Perhaps it is an example that you share with the class, or a particular video clip. Sometimes it might be a discussion question or even a graphic on a slide. Whatever it is, and no matter how small it is, having a bright spot gives you something to reach for, some part of the course that reminds you that you enjoy the topic. Consider what it might mean if you can't find a bright spot in a particular class period. Does that mean that you find the entire 50 or so minutes boring? And, if you are bored, can the students still be engaged and enriched by their time in class? Probably not.

Another way to ensure that there is enjoyment in teaching the course is to ask yourself some questions as you leave class:
• Did the students get engaged in the material today?
• Was I engaged in the material today?
• Do the students want to come back to class?
• Do I want to come back to class?

If the answer to these questions is regularly "no," consider taking the time to revise the course to add elements that will engage you and your students in a teaching and learning relationship that will inspire them to learn more and will keep you invigorated and passionate about teaching.

Chapter Seven

Closing the Feedback Loop

Once a course has been redesigned and is being taught, the concept of data-based course revision should not be forgotten. On the contrary, it should become an integral part of the course. Gathering information on how well students are learning in your class can be integrated into how you teach and how you begin planning for the next time the course is taught. This can be done as a regular aspect of teaching and doesn't necessarily require large-scale change, but indications about any needed change can be addressed. This goes beyond merely asking, "any questions?" in the last few minutes of class. In this scenario, not surprisingly, there are usually no questions and everyone seems satisfied. The faculty member is pleased that everyone in class completely understood everything that was covered and the students are happy to be able to leave class on time or even a few minutes early. This kind of questioning does not give useful data that can be used to help you make informed and meaningful decisions about redesigning a course. It most likely doesn't give any information about student learning at all—certainly none that can be used to help close the feedback loop.

As you teach a course, you will find things that need to be modified even if you don't specifically ask for information. Even faculty who don't regularly look for information on student learning and don't reflect on a class activity will find things to change in a course. Perhaps a discussion didn't go the way you wanted it to go, or maybe a new piece of information was developed that you want to add to your class.

Whatever the reason for wanting to make a change, making appropriate notes on the course as it goes along will help you when you sit down to outline the course the next time. One theatre faculty member keeps copies of lecture notes in a 3-ring binder. After each class period he jots down a note on a Post-It and sticks it to that page in the binder. At the end of the semester he goes through the binder and makes appropriate changes. Some are small matters (e.g., modification of a particular example used to describe a period costume), while others are larger issues (e.g., an assignment that was supposed to be done with group learning that didn't work well). As he revises lecture and class notes at the end of the semester, he also makes necessary modifications to the syllabus so that when it is time for classes to start, he has already done much of the work on revising this particular course. This is an easy and informal way to keep information on your course up-do-date without relying only on your memory.

Of course, there are many ways to do this. Some faculty go back after each class period and make revisions to notes or syllabi immediately. Others wait until they have more information. How you do it is up to your time schedule and the type of course revision you are planning on doing. Clearly, if you want to redesign the entire class and revise the schedule you should wait until the entire class is taught so that you can incorporate all of the changes throughout the semester. If, however, you want to just update a particular unit or one class period, this can certainly be done at any time.

COLLECTING INFORMAL FEEDBACK

Informal feedback on student engagement, satisfaction, or amounts of student learning should be gathered and reviewed on a regular basis. Feedback on student learning from exams, for example, would occur after each exam has been graded. If there are content areas or skills that students seemed to fall short on, this might be a place to consider adding more content to the unit prior to the test; conversely, if a particular test question isn't a good one, removing that item from the test bank would be an appropriate response. In addition to exams, however, there is a great deal of informal information that should be collected on all areas of the course. The following examples may stimulate you to consider additional areas in your particular course.

Mid-Semester Feedback

At various times during the semester, you will probably ask students to respond to specific questions about your course. These might be general questions concerning their learning (e.g., "What is helping you to learn in this class?" "What is hindering your learning in this class?"), or you might want specific reactions to a particular unit or assignment (e.g., "How did the research paper help you to learn more about methodology?" or "When preparing for the group presentation in class, what additional information could have helped?"). Either way, you may choose to incorporate student suggestions into the course for the future or you may want to redesign part of the course based on student responses to the mid-semester feedback.

An accounting faculty member noticed that midterm course evaluation feedback from students indicated that the in-class problems and the homework problems seemed disjointed and misaligned. The faculty member created a document that was later added to the syllabus that explained how each portion of the class built on previously learned knowledge. Students better understood the connection between the in-class problems and the homework, which helped them to see the larger learning outcomes in the class. The faculty member reported that the end-of-semester course evaluations no longer included comments from students about misalignment of activities. And, students seemed to make better use of previous examples to solve current problems. They seemed to understand the reasoning behind the structure of the course and were able to make better use of the knowledge they had already gained.

By using feedback from midterm evaluations, there is time remaining in the semester to correct misinformation or clear up confusing aspects of the course. This is an advantage of incorporating mid-semester evaluations into your course. This practice not only improves end-of-semester evaluations, but (and this is the important point) it can also give students a better focus on their own learning, which in turn increases retention of material.

When students are focusing on elements of the course that they don't like or that aren't comfortable for them, they are not paying attention to what they should learn or are actually learning. A creative writing professor was trying to get students to become more fluent in their writing and asked students to write about anything in their journals, as long as they wrote for at least 15 minutes a day. Students began to focus on the time that they were being "forced" to write. The professor admitted that the 15-minute rule was arbitrary. She was only trying to get them to write every day for several minutes. Instead, students wanted to know why it was 15 minutes instead of 10, or 20. The students were not focused on the goal of fluency of writing. They were only looking at something that they felt was unfair. The professor knew that the students were disgruntled, and she knew that they were not focusing on the fluency of their writing, but she didn't understand why. After including specific questions on a mid-semester evaluation, she discovered why they were not focusing on the writing. She modified the rule and made it much more flexible. And, she was able to better explain her rationale. Many of the students in her class became much less concerned with the time that they were writing, and instead, become more interested in the amount and the quality of their writing. Because the students and the professor were now involved in a dialogue not just about student learning but about the process of learning to write, the students were able to see the value of the activity as a means to achieve more fluent writing.

Class Period–Specific Information

When a discussion goes well in class, or students have a real "ah ha" experience and finally "get it," you may leave class feeling on top of the world. It is wonderful to know that you made a difference for a particular student or even an entire class. That difference may not be life altering on many occasions, but it may be enough to change that student's perception on a discipline-specific topic or, sometimes, about life in general.

But, sometimes you may leave class feeling that things didn't go as well as you thought they would. Students may not have been very motivated, or they may not have understood (or even done) the readings. Discussion fell flat, a demonstration didn't work, or the student presentations fell short of your expectations. By making note of these specific issues or thoughts (even without a solution), you will remember to address them later on. When making note of these things that didn't go well, it is important to be clear about what parts didn't work and any initial thoughts you have about why something didn't go well. Not only might you have a hard time reading your own handwriting later on, your cryptic note about "change that question" may not have much meaning several months later.

Making note of things that didn't go well so that they can be addressed is very important. It is a horrible déjà vu feeling to be in class doing something that you did last semester only to remember right in the middle of things that it didn't work last time, either. By making an informal, but clear, notation about the event right after it happens and keeping it with your course materials, you will avoid that experience, and making regular updates to continually improve your course will become a relatively simple process.

Class Projects or Presentations

After students submit projects, papers, or present information to the class, you generally have information about how well they learned the material and how effectively they were able to demonstrate it to the rest of the class. Did student presenters understand the material? Did the entire class seem to learn what was expected? Did the particular form of the assignment allow you to see what students know? Or, does an assignment need to be redesigned to highlight specific information or skills? Sometimes student projects or presentations fail because there wasn't a shared understanding about the teacher's expectations and the student's behavior or project. For example, if a student makes a presentation but doesn't include bibliographic information, or doesn't make appropriate audiovisuals to support the presentation, was it because it wasn't clear to the student that these were required? If that is case, then a change needs to be made to the assignment so that the expectations are clearly outlined. On the other hand, if the student failed to follow the instructions, that student should receive the appropriate, clearly communicated consequences.

An example of a modification that was made to a particular course assignment demonstrates how a simple change can make huge changes in student learning. In an introductory psychology course, a faculty member had students develop an abstracted bibliography to help them develop bibliographic skills, writing in the discipline, and to give a sense of the breadth and depth of psychological literature. However, when students turned in the final projects, the faculty member saw that many of them did not use correct APA-style citations and therefore missed many points on the assignments and, worse, did not learn what the faculty member expected them to learn. To modify this, the faculty member had students submit the first three abstracts with APA-style citations during the first three weeks of class. Students got each one back and had the opportunity to make appropriate changes. After making this simple change, the correctness of the student work increased dramatically, students demonstrated that they had learned the skill at higher levels, and students' grades improved.

Your Own Observations

Feedback and other data on your course do not always have to be quantitative and measurable by others. Most faculty regularly use informal and qualitative classroom assessment techniques. During class, for example, a faculty member asks questions like, "Did that make sense?", "Do you understand?", or makes a statement such as, "It looks like many of you are confused about this point." The responses to these can help guide the faculty member in terms of what she or he will do next. Of course, asking, "Are there any questions?" at the end of class will not usually elicit useful and engaged questions and comments. Students know that for many faculty the "any questions?" at the end of a class period is really a code for, "I'm done and you can leave early if you just say nothing."

If there is confusion in response to your questions, do you follow up on the points? Do you check again later to see if students' understanding has improved? If so, you are using informal, qualitative assessment methods to see what your students know and understand. A religion professor was talking to other faculty about students who have "ah ha" experiences in his classroom. His point was that he knew them when he saw them. But trying to quantify that and send it in as part of an overall program evaluation or departmental assessment plan was impossible. However, these "ah ha" experiences that students have are important and can be used to indicate what should stay in a course and what might need to be modified.

There are several ways to do this. One way is to record your observations after a particularly bad class period indicating what didn't seem to work or what you might change. Also, make sure to keep records about those wonderfully "ah ha"–filled class periods. Not only can these be used to lift your spirits, but you will want to make sure that you keep those activities or projects as part of the class.

Just because something is difficult or even impossible to be quantified does not mean that you cannot use it as data when you are revising a course. Teaching is both an art and science, and part of the art is that good faculty know student learning when they see it. Having said that, it is important to include multiple measures of student learning and to gather other forms of data. You don't want to base your entire course revision on your observations only—just don't be concerned about incorporating your observations into the decision-making about course revision and redesign.

EMBEDDED ASSESSMENT ITEMS

As Chapter 5 indicates, embedding information-gathering into your course is an excellent way to find out how and why students are learning without layering on additional course work for you or the students. As you are discovering, there are many creative methods to find out what students know and what they can do. Most of these can be embedded into the course and can create engagement and enhance active learning in your course. This means that you are doing two things at once: increasing the potential amount of student learning and measuring student learning. Students can apply course content to case studies, learn more, and give you insight into what they are learning.

By embedding assessment activities into your course, you are moving from thinking about "what should I teach students" to "what do I want students to learn." This admittedly simple change can modify how you approach teaching and learning in major ways! By focusing on what you want students to learn, you are really looking at whether or not they are reaching the objectives and outcomes that you have set. Using this student learning–focused paradigm, it doesn't really matter how you teach as long as the students are learning what they should and can learn.

Because of the many differences in faculty, students, and courses, some frustration can arise because no one has yet identified the "best" way to present information. Or, worse, as soon as the "best" way is identified, it is refuted by yet another study. Sometimes faculty are left wondering why they should ever even try something new or different; perhaps it is just another "fad." But when the focus is on student learning rather than on how the teacher is teaching, the changes that can occur within a course are not tied directly to any one teaching method. As a matter of fact, faculty may use even more types of teaching methodology to incorporate learning styles, use of technology, or student interests. When writing, for example, how you do it (yellow legal pad, typewriter, or the newest tablet PC) doesn't really matter. What is important is that the written document is able to be read by the expected audience. As you are reading these words, do you wonder what type of computer this author is using? Do you care? Probably not. It is the outcome that is important. So it is with student learning. The type of teaching is not as important as the learning that the teaching facilitates. And, once you know the type and amount of learning that a particular teaching method gives, you can make changes to continually enhance student learning by modifying the course.

There are many aspects of teaching and learning— the variables are almost infinite! These include teacher personality, size of the class, prior knowledge, and even time of day. By embedding activities into the course that let you know how much and what types of learning students are doing, you can continually modify your teaching methods and style to increase the probability that students will reach the learning goals and expectations that you have set. You will know earlier, rather than later, where your students are falling short and you can help to identify small problems and gaps in their learning before they become bigger problems and huge lapses in information that are difficult to fix. In addition, you get regular feedback from students about what is happening in the class. In a way, teaching a class is like driving a car. The earlier you see obstacles and bumps in the road the better you can avoid a rough ride or costly repairs at the garage.

CLOSING THE FEEDBACK LOOP

The words "closing the feedback loop" are often used in university-wide assessment offices and by visiting accreditation teams. It has become a common phrase, but many may not see the value of acting on these words. The feedback loop is the process by which outcomes are developed, measures are identified, data is collected, and then that data is used to inform the process, and it begins again with another look at the outcomes, the measures, and so forth. What unfortunately happens in many instances is that the data is collected because it is mandated. But this data is never actually used to make modifications or changes in the course or in pedagogy. Sometimes this data just sits in a dusty file drawer only to be pulled out for annual reports or the dreaded accreditation visit. Other times, the data that is collected is mined for positive statements that reaffirm the teaching process or department, leaving behind the information that could make a real difference in student learning.

To close the feedback loop, data that is collected must be evaluated and used to make decisions about the entire process (see Figure 7.1). For example, discovering that students do not understand when to use a statistical formula would indicate to a faculty member that this information should be explained again in different ways until it becomes information that students know and can use appropriately and correctly. Using data to make modifications in a class period, course design, or the sequencing of courses within a major is crucial to the ongoing development of higher education.

In addition, using the data as a lens to view the outcomes that are being measured is a critical component of assessment and course revision. As higher education moves further into the 21st century, levels of understanding, methods for obtaining knowledge, and even basic facts are changing. The outcomes that we are using to determine what students should know and do must also be examined on a regular basis to ensure that what students should be learning is what they are being asked to learn. Without closing the feedback loop, the outcomes may never be reexamined and modifications to teaching may never enhance learning.

"The classroom, then, is not a static environment . . . course design is an ongoing exploration, revealing new ways to help students achieve faculty expectations" (Cottrell & Jones, 2002, p. 7). By viewing data and the ensuing course revision as a way to help students learn, many faculty are using information on student outcomes in richer and more dynamic ways. The active learning methods that work to improve student learning in one class are being used in another class to see if they work there, too. Faculty are embracing assessment of student learning outcomes as just another facet of research, only the research is to investigate student learning in their courses. Student learning within a course is now often viewed as a dynamic relationship because of the ongoing study of student learning. Some even see "teaching and learning as more of a dialogue. Students, each with a unique life experience, and the teacher, also with a unique life experience, engage in a mutual and creative dialogue" (Magennis & Farrell, 2005, p. 46). If the paradigm is indeed moving toward teaching and learning becoming a dialogue, then judging the responses from one to the other is essential. This is the value of embedding assessment activities into the course and then using that information to close the feedback loop. Discovering what students know and using that information to enhance their learning is essential to the continued growth and development of higher education. If students are to graduate with a valuable and meaningful degree, they must be able to exist in a world that is different from the one in which current faculty were taught. Only by asking the right questions and gathering information on what should be learned and whether it is being learned can higher education prepare students not only to survive, but to thrive in their chosen discipline and in the larger world.

Figure 7.1
Closing the Feedback Loop

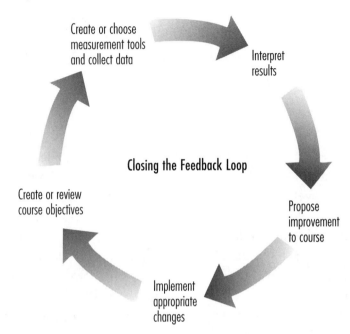

Create or choose
measurement tools
and collect data

Interpret
results

Closing the Feedback Loop

Create or review
course objectives

Propose
improvement
to course

Implement
appropriate
changes

Chapter Eight

Moving from Course-Level Decision-Making to Departmental Curriculum Planning

Once a course has been revised using student learning outcomes and other forms of data, moving from the course level to a departmental curriculum level is the next step and can add significant faculty development and enhanced student learning. The same basic steps that have been used at the course level will work by looking at the courses within the major or department. However, larger issues such as ongoing student skill enhancement, entry and exit levels of knowledge, and student preparedness can be used to assess how well students are progressing though a program of study. This is much more than senior-level program assessment! Think of a student's progression through the major in the same way that you have a student's progression through a course. There needs to be regular evaluation of student knowledge, skills, and satisfaction to know when modifications need to be made. Perhaps there are changes that need to be made in some of the introductory courses to better prepare students for advanced courses. At the macro level, making changes to the sequencing of courses, or adding a new course may be necessary to ensure that students can reach the acceptable levels of knowledge and skill as defined by the department. But how can this be done in a reasonable way? And, how can this process work within a department's already overscheduled time without unduly increasing workload demands?

As the following steps indicate, data and procedures that can be used most likely already exist. At many institutions, for example, program review is a mandated process and end-of-year reports are beginning to focus more and more on what students are learning. Since the need to document and demonstrate student learning is already required, using the process to enhance teaching and learning within the department makes sense. Unfortunately, assessment and program review are often seen as an imposition on a department from the administration rather than as a method to discover what students are learning and to develop techniques to enhance that learning. Outlined here are steps that can make the existing program review or assessment report work for the department, faculty, and students rather than just take up space in a dusty file cabinet in the administration building.

An economics department has taken steps to make the program review process work on many levels (the least important one, according to the chair, is the administrative requirement that it be submitted). The faculty were put into small groups, each looking at a different aspect of student learning and outcomes. One group was charged with examining the departmental goals for learning. They brought the existing goals to the entire department and facilitated a discussion about what each currently meant and whether or not that goal met the current needs of the department. Most of the learning goals were modified to better describe what the department wanted of its students. Another faculty group was asked to help the department explore teaching goals. As the department worked throughout the year, they were better able to clarify the outcomes for student learning and this enabled them to look more closely at the course sequencing, individual course outcomes, and teaching methods. The conversations enhanced collegiality (after a few rough early discussions) and established a new sense of trust among the department's faculty. As they await additional student learning outcome data, they plan to use this information to inform their ongoing discussions on teaching, learning, and scholarship.

MISSION STATEMENT

In order to be explicit about the outcomes that a department's or program's students should reach, a clear statement of mission and objectives should be outlined. Many departments already have a mission statement, but even if it isn't a formal and published description, having all of the faculty agree that students should be able to perform specific tasks is essential to developing the ongoing conversation regarding department-level curriculum design. However, sometimes having this department-wide discussion can be difficult. In order to make this process meaningful, the discussion of the mission statement should take place in the context of clarifying what students are learning and using that information to inform the ongoing departmental discussions.

One method to get the conversation started is to ask the entire faculty to briefly describe, in writing or any other method, the ideal graduating student in the department. What abilities does this student have? What skills can she or he demonstrate? What ethical beliefs are held? In what activities has this ideal graduating senior participated? And, what elements of your program have been a part of the development of this student over the undergraduate years? Asking these types of questions will have the faculty looking at outcomes that are meaningful, somewhat measurable, and philosophically relevant to the faculty. The goal is to have them think not about what content they teach in class, but about what students are actually learning and doing. For example, a faculty member in an English department outlined issues relating to what texts students had read, the methods by which they critiqued others' writing, and the fact that students valued the written word. In this language, it becomes clear that developing a meaningful measure of how much a student values something is difficult. But, when this information came to the full department, it turned out that many faculty agreed with her and they began to talk about what a student who values reading would do. They developed a method to ask students to list the last three books they read and other measures that asked for a satisfaction ranking on several reading items. While this may not be the perfect measure, it got the department talking about how to encourage students to value reading. This ongoing dialogue caused several faculty to add to their courses reflection papers on issues relating to the value of reading a particular assignment or text.

By coming to an agreement about what the ideal graduate should be like, your department is developing, or at least clarifying, the outcomes that students should meet. These are similar to the outcomes that you have for any particular course, just broader to encompass more information, skills, and abilities. The ideal-student discussion should take place over time, not rushed into during a single one-hour time period, but the duration depends on the size of your department and the level of agreement prior to the conversations. Keep in mind that the dimensions of the ideal student are just the beginning of the discussion on the department's overall student learning outcomes. It is likely that many students who graduate are not the ideal student and that the outcomes developed by the department may reflect minimum qualifications rather than the ideal. This is fine because the discussion is at least happening and will continue to occur given the need.

Development of Student Learning Outcomes

Leading from the ideal-student discussion into the development of specific outcomes can be a straightforward process. Depending on your department, this discussion may take place without any difficulties and the transition from the ideal student into outcomes may flow freely. If not, there are ways to foster this discussion. One way is to ask each faculty member to think back to her or his responses to the ideal student questions and from these, develop a list of two to three objectives. For example, if the ideal student in an education program is one who can appropriately apply Piaget's (1950) theory to a complex case study, one outcome might be, "Students in the education program will be able to correctly identify the Piagetian stage in a case study and outline appropriate teacher behaviors that correspond with the developmental needs of the student in the case study."

After all faculty members have had the opportunity to list their top outcomes, list all of them together. You will find that many are similar, and these will probably garner the highest level of agreement. In most cases you will not find perfect agreement. Focus on the big picture areas, but make sure that all important areas are covered in some way. At this point you may decide to allow faculty to add other objectives that don't necessarily come from the ideal-student responses but are still considered important objectives. This ensures that the list of objectives is more complete and covers areas that need to be learned by students in your department.

After there is general agreement on these outcomes (and you will probably have to hold some back that do not reach consensus or a majority agreement), these objectives can easily be translated into outcome statements. Keep in mind that you will later be measuring what students know or can demonstrate, so a clear understanding of what is being asked in these outcomes is essential. Clearing up misconceptions or unclear statements should be done as soon as the misconception is identified. While this may prolong the initial discussion, it will certainly simplify the process later on.

DETERMINING WHEN SPECIFIC OUTCOMES SHOULD BE MET

After creating a list of student learning outcomes, the task of determining when they should be met is at hand. Which courses should meet which outcomes? How many courses should meet the same outcomes? By developing a matrix of courses and outcomes, it becomes easy to see which courses should address specific outcomes. This doesn't mean that these outcomes are the only ones to be addressed by any means! A course has specific content in addition to overall departmental outcomes. The development of course outcomes should include course-specific and appropriate department-specific outcomes (often with overlap between these two categories). For example, a social psychology course has content that is specific to social psychology and has outcomes that are different from other psychology courses. However, the social psychology course may also address issues related to research design and might address some department-level outcome as well as the course-specific social psychology outcomes.

The creation of a matrix can be useful to all faculty within a department but can be especially useful to new faculty or to those who are teaching a new course. By seeing which departmental outcomes should be addressed in the course, a new faculty member will have a more clear picture of how that course fits into the overall sequencing of courses within the major or program. This can also be very helpful in the identification of prerequisite courses as it explicitly identifies the skills or knowledge that a student should gain from the successful completion of the prerequisite course.

SHARING OBJECTIVES WITH STUDENTS

Much of the discussion of student learning outcomes, departmental measures, and course decision-making has left out a very important element—the student. One of the paradoxes in the relatively recent assessment movement in higher education is that much of the data comes from students, but is not designed to have any benefit to the students. This is an unfortunate oversight and an important missed opportunity to enhance student learning:

> Assessment [of student learning outcomes] should be seen as a teaching tool. When the criteria for assessment are made public, faculty, students, and future students (as well as employers) can readily see the requirements and outcomes of your program. This will allow students to know more clearly where they stand in the department and will encourage

them to take responsibility for their own learning and to see their advisor or another faculty member if they are missing an important piece of the criteria. (Wehlburg, 2001, p. 28)

There are many different methods for sharing departmental expectations with students. For example, your department could begin listing them in public places within the department or put them in departmental curricular brochures or catalogues. Your department might consider including the outcomes in information that goes to students as they become majors in your program. Or, the department could have students measure their own progress in terms of how they have met your department's outcomes. This becomes another use of the matrix discussed earlier. For example, one department asks students to comment on their progress toward each objective at specific times of the academic year (first day of classes, advising times, and the end of a senior capstone course).

By frequently discussing how the outcomes fit into the overall curricular design of your major, faculty may develop additional department-specific methods for sharing outcomes with students and other important populations. "Creating a culture where learning outcomes are part of the educational cycle will strengthen the department by strengthening the students who graduate" (Wehlburg, 2001, p. 28).

COLLECTING INFORMATION ON SPECIFIC OBJECTIVES

Once the decisions have been made about the content of specific objectives and the matrix of courses and the outcomes expected from those courses developed, the decisions regarding what information will be gathered need to be made. As faculty in your department discussed what the ideal student should be like, discussions about how to measure ideal behaviors probably arose. The difficulty in this is that not all objectives and outcomes are easily and meaningfully measured: "Assessment per se guarantees nothing by way of improvement; no more than a thermometer cures a fever" (Marchese, 1987, p. 3). However, gathering information on what students are learning, even if that doesn't give the entire picture, is still necessary in terms of gathering data to revise a course or curriculum.

Unfortunately, faculty sometimes find a measurement tool to use before considering what aspects of student behavior or learning need to be measured. For example, a biology department decides to use a nationally standardized test that measures general biology knowledge. This can give insightful information about what students know if it is used appropriately. But, perhaps the information comes back and the average student scores in the 70th percentile. What does this mean? What specific parts of biology do students know? What parts are they missing? A single nationally standardized test score can give useful data to a department, but only if it is used to measure specific outcomes. Unfortunately, this type of data often ends up being relatively useless to a department that is interested in discovering what students know and what they don't know so that the department's curriculum can be revised and enhanced.

Looking at the overall objectives for your department and the course(s) in which those might be met, you can get a general picture of the range of possibilities for measuring what students know and the behaviors and skills that they can demonstrate. Certainly, many departments use a nationally standardized (or even a locally developed) instrument to measure student knowledge. These can be very useful, but also consider using existing data. For example, in the courses that are thought to address a specific outcome, is there an assignment that could be added to a student portfolio? Is there an assignment that could be included in several courses? In a psychology department that teaches several sections of introduction to psychology per semester (taught by several different faculty members), faculty decided to include a particular paper assignment in all sections that would be used to measure knowledge of APA-style writing. This enabled the entire department to look at student skills across the department, rather than individual faculty members' courses through their own assignments. Thus, one outcome was measured by work done in class. Using a particular measurement (in this case, the paper assignment) for two purposes saves time and becomes part of the multiple measures of a specific outcome.

Using multiple measures of any given outcome is important because any item on an instrument or test only samples a very small piece of information. It may take several items or measures to get closer to an accurate picture of what a student knows. As you collect these multiple measures, you are able to see "patterns of convergence in data that can be used to make appropriate educational and programmatic changes" (Revak & Scheffel, 2001, p. 229).

As faculty discuss methods of gathering information on student behaviors, skills, and knowledge, they will also be deciding how these will be demonstrated. For example, if you want to see how well a student follows laboratory safety guidelines, you could give a multiple-choice quiz, an essay question, or a visual demonstration of proper procedure. It is up to the department to determine what best meets their needs. There are innovative ways to create assignments and measurements of student learning outcomes. Most departments that begin this discussion continue to talk about innovative assignments that enhance student learning at the time they are assigned and can then be used to assess student learning across the department.

Identifying Other Sources of Data

There are a variety of sources that can be used to discover what students know. There are many nationally normed tests that can be purchased and administered to students as part of their education. For example, those students in a Nursing B.A. program must take a national exam to receive licensure. All students take this exam at the end of their educational program. This information can be used by the department to determine whether or not what the students are learning is appropriate. If not, changes can be made to the program. There are also locally developed instruments that measure overall student learning and are often given as part of a capstone course. Again, this information can be used to look at the level of student learning at the end of a particular major.

Individual assignments within existing courses can also be used to determine the level of student learning. An advantage of discovering information at this level is that changes can occur that can positively impact the current student. For example, if a course is supposed to teach APA-style writing, but less than 40% of the students can appropriately cite information by the end of the course, a department can choose to add additional information about APA writing into other courses. In other words, this type of data can be used in a formative way that will help the individual student, but the aggregate data can inform the faculty within the department about what areas need to be revised.

A department might decide to use anchored exam items. This category of exams has common items in them which will allow the department to compare a student performance over several semesters on these particular items that correspond to the departmental outcomes. Revak and Scheffel (2001) indicate that because there are common exam items in anchored exams, "benchmarking is easily accomplished immediately after the closeout of the semester" (p. 231).

Beyond exams and papers, a department might decide to incorporate authentic measures of student learning. Often called *authentic assessment*, this type of measurement should "mirror applications of the assessed ability in real-life, nonacademic settings" (Davies & Wavering, 1999, p. 40). These types of measurements are being used more and more in higher education, because they can enhance student learning in an assignment and can also be used to look at overall student performance levels. Using alternative assessment methods can also allow for learning-style differences among students in your department. Gardner's (1983) work on multiple intelligences has helped to identify a need for a variety of measurement formats. In agreement with Gardner's concept, Wiggins (1989) has said that "mass testing, as we know it, treats students as objects—as if their education and thought processes were similar and as if the reasons for their answers were irrelevant" (p. 708). Therefore, adding measures that are more authentic can enable the department to see more clearly what students know and can do. Where there are elements lacking in students' knowledge base, faculty can make decisions about where information should be added or what aspects of curricular design should be modified, deleted, or enhanced.

Using alternative assessment methods will also create the opportunity for the student to use higher-level thinking skills resulting in higher-level thinking in student work.

> If the ability to engage in complex reasoning is a desired outcome of higher education, assessments should challenge students to problem solve, make connections, explore assumptions, elaborate, and apply non-algorithmic thinking. Multiple-choice tests hold limited capacity to assess more complex thinking and do not assess interests, attitudes, growth, or connective reasoning. (Davies & Wavering, 1999, p. 42)

A department may decide to include several pieces of student work in order to measure multiple objectives. In this case, a portfolio of student products may be a choice for the collection of data. A portfolio is a "purposeful collection of student work that exhibits the student's efforts, progress, and/or achievements. The collection must include student participation in selecting contents, the criteria for selection, the criteria for judging merit, and evidence of student self-reflection" (Paulson, Paulson, & Meyer, 1991, p. 60). Of course, many departments have used portfolios for a variety of purposes for centuries. Almost all students who major in one of the fine arts must complete several items that will go into a portfolio for job searching or to demonstrate skill. A benefit of the use of portfolios to document student work over the course of several semesters is that it can be personalized to meet the specific needs of the student and the department. To measure students' knowledge and skill level using a portfolio, many departments assign them in an early course (an introduction course or one of the first courses required by majors) to be handed in as part of a capstone course. At a liberal arts college, portfolios have been used to measure general education outcomes. Students are given a handout that outlines the components of the portfolio at the beginning of their first year on campus. Working with their advisors, they choose the elements of the portfolio over a four-year time period and submit it just prior to graduation. This process has many benefits: It can lead to the student having a much better understanding of the purpose of a particular program and it can give the faculty rich and detailed information about the overall student knowledge and how students are meeting (or not meeting) specific outcomes.

In addition to these direct measures of student learning, there are other more indirect methods of discovering what students know and can do. For example, great insight can be gained from recent graduates about what information they needed to have to be successful in their chosen career path. Interviewing or surveying recent alumni can give a department a different view of what students know and can do. Asking alumni about what elements in your program were important, what areas they feel should have been focused on in greater detail, or in what areas they felt unprepared, can give the department a very important perspective on student learning. It is possible that the alumni office at your institution has a database of recent graduates and they might even be able to help in collecting this information.

Consider asking questions of the employers of your recent graduates. While this may not give you the kind of rich data that you get from your graduates (many employers do not have the time to share much information), it can still give you information about the areas your students are performing well in and which areas might be lacking. One business college has discovered that employers wanted students to develop more effective group and team skills and that the recent graduates came in with a lot of book information but not enough actual experience working in project groups. The college wouldn't have known this if they hadn't asked the employers what skill students were not prepared to demonstrate. Similarly, a computer science department discovered that students were not well prepared to work with multiple types of clients. In response to this data, they incorporated a course that was linked to an entrepreneurial course in another department. The computer science students had to work with the entrepreneurial students (the "client") to support their project. This gave both classes an opportunity to become more involved in their learning and to engage with the material in a variety of ways.

By using existing measures of student learning and by adding other elements that measure outcomes that are specific to your department, you will be able to gather meaningful data that will enable modifications in curriculum and course sequencing at the department level. As long as the discussions about measurements and the meaningfulness of the measures are part of the ongoing collegial discussions, these measurements will give faculty the information they need to continue to enhance student learning by revising the program of study. But moving from looking at collected data to actually making recommendations for change can be challenging. The following section focuses on how to use the data to make appropriate curricular decisions.

USING DATA TO MAKE DEPARTMENTAL CURRICULAR DECISIONS

Biggs (1999) discusses the impact that outcomes have on teaching and student learning: "Here is a design for good teaching: When we have decided what we want students to learn, we teach and assess accordingly" (p. 11). This deceptively simple, but very accurate, description of the process can be applied to individual courses or to the program of study within a given major.

Once data is collected, the department must make decisions regarding the meaning of the information and the level of curricular revision that is indicated. It is important to have department-wide discussions, rather than limiting the discussions to a select group of faculty. By involving faculty in this process, you can ensure that faculty will want to see and appropriately use the information on student learning.

It is extremely important to ensure that the discussions on the data and objectives stay at the department level and do not spread into discussions of an individual course or an individual faculty member. If this occurs, the discussion can quickly degenerate into a "blaming the other" discussion and meaningful curricular change can never begin. The responsibility of student learning at the department level is shared by all faculty. Encourage discussion throughout the process so that all faculty have some sense of ownership over the process.

Once the groundwork has been laid, the discussions about outcomes and measurements have occurred, and data has been collected, it is time to begin by looking at the objectives and their corresponding data in order to determine which seem to be met by "enough" students. What does "enough" mean to your department? Is it a percentage amount (at least 80% of students can _____)? These decisions should already have been made before discussion of the actual data. Of course, it is entirely possible that in looking at the data faculty determine that the original benchmarks or criteria are not appropriate. Modifying those in order to refine the information can be a meaningful step in the process. Make certain, however, that these discussions are happening because of a need to clarify the data and not just to make a department or division "look good." It can be difficult to have these discussions without causing "turf protecting," but it is essential to keep the focus on what the ideal student should know. Encourage everyone to consider curricular changes indicated by the data that will enhance student learning. All faculty are part of the larger department and can affect students. An analogy of the role of the faculty member who might, as a result of the data on student learning, make changes in a course is given below:

> This is a story about a little wave, bobbing along on the ocean, having a grand old time. He's enjoying the wind and the fresh air— until he notices the other waves in front of him, crashing against the shore.

> "This is terrible," the wave says. "Look what's gong to happen to me!" Then along comes another wave. It sees the first wave, looking grim, and it says to him, "Why do you look so sad?"

> The first wave says, "You don't understand! We're all going to crash! All of us waves are going to be nothing! Isn't it terrible?"

The second wave says, "No, you don't understand. You're not a wave, you're part of the
ocean." (Albom, 1997, pp. 179–180)

As a unified department working toward the
enhancement of student learning, discussion of curricular
revision and pedagogical modifications can be an opportunity for faculty development and improved student
learning. This is not an opportunity to be missed! When
faculty can see that these discussions and the work of
using data to make curricular decisions at the department
level do have an impact and are meaningful discussions,
the focus moves from thinking that this adds more work
to already straining schedules to realizing that these
discussions make the work that is already being done
more meaningful and potentially more time efficient. In
addition, problems of student learning can begin to be
more proactively addressed. For example, consider the
shock and surprise to learn that a higher percentage of
students than usual did not pass a certification exam in an
applied field—how much better it would have been to
measure students' learning and focus on areas of concern
early on rather than waiting to discover this at the end of
the senior year. These discussions on student learning
and pedagogy are crucial and should be a part of ongoing
departmental agendas, hallway conversations, and end-of-
year reporting.

CONCLUSION

Moving from a data-based course revision process to a
department-level process can be daunting and challenging
by almost any standard; however, the benefit to students,
faculty, and the entire educational process cannot be over-
stated. Students benefit in the classroom, because their

learning is focused on what is important to their specific discipline. Students also increase their responsibility for learning and many come to view their educational process as a relationship rather than as what the faculty must "do" to them. In addition, faculty gain understanding about how and why students learn and can explore alternative teaching methods and assessment strategies. These discussions add to the depth of faculty teaching and can enhance already good teaching styles. Also, alumni will benefit because the information and skills that they gained during their time in your department will be maximized and even more meaningful. Finally, the entire institution could gain increased understanding of the ongoing discussions of teaching and learning and how these discussions can actually move an institution toward a culture that uses data to inform many decisions, not just teaching-related decisions.

Chapter Nine

Creating a Culture of Student Learning Outcomes Assessment

*F*aculty comments about assessment often sound something like this:

> Assessment? I am not sure what all this emphasis is about, but we do lots of assessment here. I grade my students, they evaluate me after each course, and every five or six years my department gets reviewed. Isn't that enough? Why are people asking for more? (Wolff & Harris, 1994, p. 271).

When most academics hear the word "assessment" several thoughts come to mind, and most are not very pleasant! In many instances, assessment has come to mean a specific hoop through which a department must jump in order to please institution-wide assessment committees and accreditation agencies. As a matter of fact, the first chapter in McTighe Musil's (1992) book on feminist assessment is titled "Relax Your Neck Muscles." Assessment of student learning has been around for as long as people have been learning. At the very basic level, consider what happens when you talk with students about a concept from class. You judge how much they know from their facial expressions, the type of questions that they ask, and their responses to your questions. When it seems that they don't understand the concept, you go back over an issue, try other examples, or direct them to specific resources in order to get them to understand the information. This is assessment in a nutshell.

It has, however, taken on a much more complex process as it has been institutionalized, but the basic principles remain the same:

• Determine what you want students to know, to be, and to be able to do as a result of graduating from your institution.
• Consider what information you need to see in order to determine if the students have learned the information.
• Look at the data that you get and the data that you may have already collected.
• Use that data to make decisions about educational and institutional issues.

By first determining what you want students to know, you are designing the outcomes against which you will measure student learning. According to the American Association for Higher Education (1992):

> The assessment of student learning begins with educational values. Assessment is not an end in itself but a vehicle for educational improvement. Its effective practice, then, begins with and enacts a vision of the kinds of learning we most value for students and strive to help them achieve. (p. 2)

By considering what issues and values your institution holds, you can determine how you want to go about assessing what students know and can do. Because these can occur at the institutional level, the mission statement of your institution can take a very meaningful role. "Assessment can have a profound transformational impact on an institution" (Magruder, McManis, & Young,

1997, p. 17). The mission statement at many institutions is mostly seen as window dressing—nice words that sound great when mentioned at graduation ceremonies or opening convocations. But an institution's mission statement is generally a statement of the institution's core values and beliefs. By using the mission as a place to begin considering an institutional assessment program, you can integrate the assessment into what is already occurring on campus and make the data that is collected meaningful and something that individuals and departments will use.

The American Association for Higher Education (AAHE, 1992) also states, "assessment is most effective when it reflects an understanding of learning as multidimensional, integrated, and revealed in performance over time" (p. 2). This aspect of assessment is crucial if the data that you get is to be valuable. For example, one institution began to assess student learning by looking at graduation rates. This can give some information, but it doesn't really measure student learning directly. The institution in this example found that no one really cared about the assessment results. It wasn't until the assessment questions started to look at what students were learning and how they were demonstrating it that faculty and departments started to look at the information and use it in meaningful ways. Student learning is complex: There are many ways to measure it, and faculty and departments have different perspectives on it. It is "analogous to the experience of admiring the geometric figures in an M.C. Escher drawing. The meaning and impact of the experience are very different for each observer" (Banta, Lund, Black, & Oblander, 1996, p. 10). This does not, however, mean that assessment can't give data that can be used by a large number of people. It can. But the assessment questions that are asked should take into account that learning is a complex concept to measure and cannot be reasonably assessed by one single test or behavior.

In growing a culture of assessment, those involved must begin with the mission statement and use the values of the institution to create outcomes or standards against which you can measure student behavior. Not everything can be measured. Some elements (good citizenship, for example) are very difficult to measure directly and require several indirect measures. As a matter of fact, it may prove impossible to measure everything. In developing a culture of assessment, it is actually best not even to try to measure everything. Start with the values and beliefs, start small, and start with the aspects of student learning and behavior that are most important to the institution. Assessment planning will always be a work in progress. Ideally, student learning will increase, so the assessment target is moving continuously.

Because of this changing target, "assessment works best when it is ongoing, not episodic" (AAHE, 1992, p. 2). Institutions should begin to look at student learning as something that evolves over time, not something that is learned in a single event: "Successful assessment is an ongoing, iterative process" (Banta, Lund, Black, & Oblander, 1996, p. 29). Asking questions about the data should be a regular occurrence. Why did we get these results? What does this mean? What happens if . . . ? By seeing this process as dynamic and informative rather than reactive and sterile, assessment planning can become a part of the institutional culture and move and change as needed. This is the real purpose of assessment—showing what learning is happening and where it is not in order to make appropriate modifications that can bring students where the institution wants them to be and to make data-based institutional decisions that will enhance the mission of the institution.

BENEFITS OF A CULTURE OF ASSESSMENT

With a culture of assessment and data-based decision-making, several important things can happen. The institution can build a shared understanding of the values that are held and the outcomes that are expected. In addition, institutional decision-making becomes more transparent and all involved can see why decisions are made. Furthermore, decisions that are made are based on information that is important to the institution, its faculty, staff, and students because they have already been agreed upon and are part of the institutional culture. The information from an assessment can then be used a variety of ways. For example, Truman State University has experienced "profound changes" as a result of institutionalizing assessment efforts (Magruder, McManis, & Young, 1997). The types of changes that might occur on your campus will vary, but when an institution seriously considers using information about what students are learning and doing, that institution is better prepared to meet the needs of students in an ever-changing world.

According to Lakos and Phipps (2004), several areas indicate that a culture of assessment exists on a campus, including:

• The organization's mission, planning, and policies are focused on the needs of those who use the services. In most cases, this means that the focus is on student learning, faculty teaching, and institutional programming.

• An indication of how performance measures will be assessed is included in organizational documents. For

example, in a recently developed general education
curriculum, the focus areas included student learning
outcome statements and action steps. This creates a
system in which faculty know what students should
learn, students can see what they need to know and do,
and the institution can more easily assess the outcome
since it was created along with the description and outline of the general education curriculum.

- Institutional leadership is committed to assessment
activities and uses the data for decision-making. This
also includes a budgetary commitment. Support of these
activities can be seen in organizational structure, faculty
committees, and institutional decision-making processes.

- Faculty and staff see the value of assessment and incorporate these activities into what they do. Faculty and
staff contracts and organizational roles are formally
outlined and used. "Assessment should become part of
the everyday work process. It needs to become part of
the decision-making loop in the organization, a normal
part of evaluating internal processes" (Lakos & Phipps,
2004, p. 353).

- Data are routinely collected and used to "set priorities,
allocate resources, and make decisions" (Lakos &
Phipps, 2004, p. 353). In order for an assessment program
to become part of the institutional culture, the data that
is used must be collected and shared on a regular basis.
Then, that data must be used in meaningful and appropriate ways to make enhancements or changes to
improve student learning. Planning processes should be
in place that regularly gather data and share it with
appropriate constituents. At one campus, data had been
collected for years but was never shared widely. When
the faculty learned about the "new" data, they were

excited and wanted to see more of it. Faculty were very surprised to discover that there was a great deal of information about student learning that they could use to determine whether what they were doing was really teaching students what they intended. The dusty file drawers and neglected computer files of data were pulled out and analyzed; requests for ongoing assessment data increased. In addition, the type of conversation on campus changed. Faculty meetings contained discussions of teaching and learning. New data points were analyzed and questioned. The culture of the institution moved to talking about teaching and learning from an assessment perspective. Student learning became an important aspect of regular discussion and end-of-year reports. An institutionalized culture of assessment is

> an organizational environment in which decisions are based on facts, research, and analysis, and where services are planned and delivered in ways that maximize positive outcomes and impacts . . . a culture of assessment exists in organizations where staff care to know what results they produce and how these results relate to expectations. (Lakos & Phipps, 2004, p. 352)

The benefits are in the integrated conversations and institutional planning processes that revolve around information that comes from assessment information. As the integration deepens, the climate becomes more focused on intentional student learning rather than on reactive teacher behaviors or decisions that might be based on administrative whims.

POSSIBLE OBSTACLES TO BUILDING A CULTURE OF ASSESSMENT

Assessment is a moral activity. What we choose to assess and how shows quite starkly what we value. In assessing these aspects of chemistry or by assessing German in that way, we are making it abundantly clear what we value in this programme and in higher education in general. So, if we choose not to assess general transferable skills, then it is an unambiguous sign that promoting them is not seen to be an important part of our work. (Knight, 1995, p. 13)

One of the first obstacles to creating a culture of assessment is that it requires the institution to clearly state its values. What is assessed is what becomes important because that is what students, faculty, and the public will focus on.

If you look across your campus right now, there are already many aspects of the institution that are being assessed: development funding, grant funding, numbers of students admitted, and student retention rate. There may not have been a campus-wide discussion on these issues, but these are being measured, and therefore are focused upon by the institution. However, what is often missing is an overarching focus on assessing student learning that is broader than and escapes the disciplinary, departmental space.

Of course, individual faculty assess student learning and some use this information to modify and revise their courses. This is wonderful! And, as the focus of this book indicates, this is an important method to use for revising a course. Some departments also use assessment to enhance what students are learning in the major, make modifications to course sequencing, and demonstrate overall student learning within the department. This is a meaningful and significant use of assessment data! But asking an entire institution to use information about student learning and student behavior can be a daunting task, fraught with political and practical battles. Just trying to get faculty to identify meaningful ways to assess cross-departmental programs such as general education can be very difficult and time consuming. Adding the entire campus to the discussion is very hard. After all, getting all (or even most) constituents to answer the question, "What is special about a degree from our institution?" is difficult at best. But the efforts are worthwhile and the outcomes can be transformative to the institution!

TRANSFORMING AN
INSTITUTION'S CULTURE

Knight (1995) discusses assessment as being at the heart of an "integrated approach" to learning. Without the information that comes from meaningful assessment data, there is no way to know what students are learning, how they are learning, or what they are lacking in knowledge and skills. And, if you don't know what students are learning, it is very difficult to know what needs to be modified so that student learning can improve. Assessment should be at the heart of higher education. We should look to the data on student learning to inform our decisions, to guide our teaching methods, and to ensure that our institutions are making good on the promises and expectations for our students.

Even the process of discussing an institutional assessment program can be transformative. On almost any level, the discussion about what should be learned, what students should be able to demonstrate, and where the campus should be is crucial. At one institution, the faculty began with a discussion about the assessment of general education. While at first, this seemed a relatively defined discussion, it turned into a year-long, intense, developmental discussion about what the key aspects of a degree from the institution were. Faculty had to come to a consensus on what was important for students to learn. This discussion alone was worth all of the problems that are inherent with the issues. When a cross-departmental committee got together to discuss the outcomes for general education and hammered out a listing (after many meetings), the resulting discussions allowed real focus on learning and the teaching that preceded that learning. Faculty were able to see past a checklist of courses and look for outcomes that included skills and knowledge. These outcomes then had to be measured. Carefully defining and choosing appropriate measurement tools was essential and created a culture in which faculty considered student learning to be first priority.

The discussion, planning, and consensus-building aspect of these conversations can certainly be transformative. It is important to note, however, that if these decisions are imposed from an administrator to the faculty, the transformative nature of the culture of assessment is lost. And, worse, the use of data for the purpose of enhancing teaching and learning will, most likely, not occur. Faculty will see this as "yet another" program that is being added to the things they must do. However, if the time needed can be allowed, the discussions on student learning and assessment will create a new climate on campus. "Faculty cannot simply be told that assessment is important, meaningful, and full of insight for their teaching" (Driscoll & Wood, 2004); they must be able to create the process that aligns the course work and other student behaviors with institutional outcomes.

A very important aspect of creating this new climate is to put the assessment plan into place. It is amazing when faculty can see data about student learning and discover things that they didn't know before about how students are learning across campus. Critical thinking, for example, is often seen by institutions as an important goal. But is it really taught? Do students learn how to do this? And, how do we know that they have learned this? When a measurement tool is used to measure an outcome reliably and appropriately, the data becomes useful and critical thinking (or whichever skill is being examined) becomes more than a nice concept. Faculty begin to talk about how to increase student skills in this area, they share pedagogy, and they might participate in campus-wide workshops or discussions on the topic. The "walls" that often surround an individual faculty member's classroom may come down and student learning becomes the important outcome. Faculty may begin to look for new teaching methods that measure student learning in authentic ways. These transformative conversations and actions can make major changes in the culture of an institution.

Who Should Be Involved?

The process of using assessment to transform an institutional culture should involve all relevant stakeholders. Faculty, staff, and administration, of course, should be deeply involved in the early discussions. But others should also be involved, including students, alumni, and community members. All constituencies will bring slightly different issues and thoughts to the table and these will help make the final assessment plan truly transformative. After all, helping students achieve what the institution says that they should is important to all involved.

Even though these initial conversations are very time-consuming and can be extremely frustrating, they are essential to begin to build the foundation upon which a unique assessment plan for a specific institution can be built. While there are many aspects of higher education that are shared by all institutions, there are specific institutional, regional, traditional, and historical differences among them. These differences must be included in each institution's assessment culture. In order for these unique aspects of the institution to be included in the initial discussions, members from all areas of the institutional community should be included.

ACCREDITATION ISSUES

Assessment, in order to be successful and meaningful, cannot begin because of an upcoming accreditation visit. Assessment planning and data use should be ongoing and continuous processes designed for the explicit purpose of enhancing learning at the institution. Consider this rough analogy: Most people will clean their houses prior to expected guests arriving. This is a normal response and something that wouldn't shock most. But, do you do major renovation on your house just because guests are expected? Or, does the major renovation take place because your family needs more space or an additional garage? Accreditation visits are like expected guests coming into your home. You may not want them to stay a long time and you will probably tidy up your home just before they walk in the door. But to consider major renovation just because they are coming would seem pretty extreme.

Rather, the accreditation teams should see what is really happening at the institution.

Unfortunately, the uses of assessment ramp up in the two to three years prior to a visit from a regional accreditation team. Reports and checklists are submitted, and all such things are done only because of the approaching visit. The problem with this is that it is being done for all the wrong reasons. The most important purpose of assessment is not accountability to an outside observer. The purpose of institutional assessment should be to discover how well students are reaching the goals of the institution and to modify the methods for attaining these goals when students fall short. If an institution is doing this, the accreditation visit becomes one in which the team can see what students are learning, can give consultative advice when needed, and can see the data that has already been gathered. Assessment was not designed to be used simply for accountability. It was and is meant for determining where students are on the outcomes that are important to that institution so that any necessary modifications can be identified and implemented.

While few in higher education would admit to looking forward to a visiting team from an accreditation association, it does provide the opportunity to do some mopping up (to continue with the house-cleaning analogy). This can be a very useful task and can help the entire institution to revisit the methods that it is using to document the outcomes being measured, among other aspects of an accreditation visit. It also gives the higher education community the means to ensure that all institutions are meeting basic standards and requirements. When an institution is not meeting the standards, it is essential that monitoring of that institution take place.

While accreditation visits could be seen as an opportunity to "clean house" and get ready for company, highlighting things that are going well and modifying those that aren't, we don't need to wait for it to do these things. We can, and should, be using assessment of student learning regularly, regardless of when the next visit is scheduled. By making assessment planning and programming part of the institutional culture, it becomes much more meaningful and can be a positive catalyst for appropriate and important change.

CHARACTERISTICS OF AN INSTITUTIONAL CULTURE OF ASSESSMENT

Institutions that have successfully created a meaningful and shared culture of assessment have certain characteristics.

- There is a shared understanding across campus about the purpose of the institution and how student learning fits into the overall institutional priorities.
- Goals of the institution take into account the data from assessment activities, and decision-making is relatively transparent and closely related to the outcomes.
- Improvement is not looked upon as a one-time event. It is continuous and all view enhancement and improvement as ever-increasing goals and outcomes.
- Discussions, while they may be heated, still allow for diverse viewpoints and possibilities. Different ideas and directions are focused on increasing quality, rather than on protecting turf.
- There is significant endorsement of ongoing, regular, and meaningful collaboration among administrators, faculty, staff, and (often) students.
- The organizational structure of the institution allows for and promotes regular interdepartmental discussions of

the goals of the assessment program. This structure includes appropriate support units for the necessary functions of the institution.

- The reward structure is designed to take into consideration work that is being done toward institutional goals and outcomes. The belief that appropriate and meaningful assessment will improve research, teaching, and other elements necessary to the functioning of the institution is shown by the recognition system that is in place.

- Acculturation of new faculty, staff, administrators, and students is done in a way that outlines the expectations and processes of the institution. "It provides a comprehensive introduction and operational definition of student learning–centered" institutional functioning (Lee, Mentkowski, Drout, McGury, Hamilton, & Shapiro, 2003, p. 14).

- The institution uses results of the assessment plan to communicate with all constituents including parents, alumni, community, and a national audience.

CONCLUSION

The assessment process within an institution, department, or individual course follows basic principles that are very much related to how students learn. After all, in class students are presented with information and are asked to apply it and modify their original cognitive constructs. Using assessment data is very similar. Race (1995) talks about how people learn best; these learning factors include:

- The importance of 'the want to learn,' or motivation

- The fact that most learning is 'by doing,' including practice, and trial and error

- The importance of receiving feedback from other people

- The need to make sense of what has been learned, or to 'digest' it (p. 61)

These factors can also be applied to the faculty and institutional staff learning about how well students are meeting objectives. In order for the assessment process to work, the institution must have faculty and staff who have the motivation to take part in the early assessment discussions and to see that the information will be essential and useful to them (rather than being used as a potential source of punishment). They then must be able to create the means to gather information, choose the measurement tools, and be a part of designing the assessment plan. The information that results from the assessment process can then be used by the faculty and staff and they can see how the data might show a need for revision of pedagogy, sequencing of courses or events, or even the initially stated outcomes. Finally, the entire institution must be able to see the assessment results and how they are integrated into the larger institutional picture. When this can be done across campus, faculty, students, staff, community members, and alumni can have a much richer and deeper understanding of the meaning of the mission statement and can be reasonably proud of the role that they played in the entire process.

This is how the creation of a culture of assessment can be transformative. The entire campus can be involved in various parts of the process and can see the results of the work that has been done. All constituents can take pride in the students that graduate from the institution and the great things that alumni will do.

Suggested Readings

Bain, K. (2004). *What the best college teachers do.* Cambridge, MA: Harvard University Press.

Biggs, J. (2003). *Teaching for quality learning* (2nd ed.). Philadelphia, PA: Society for Research into Higher Education and Open University Press.

Borg, J. R., & Borg, M. O. (2001). Teaching critical thinking in interdisciplinary economics courses. *College Teaching, 49*(1), 20–25.

Christoffersen, S. (2002). An active learning tool for the principles of economics: The allocation exercise. *American Economist, 46*(2), 65–68.

Felder, R. M., & Brent, R. (2001). Effective Strategies for Cooperative Learning. *Journal of Cooperation & Collaboration in College Teaching, 10*(2), 69–75.

Gupta, G. (2005). Improving students' critical-thinking, logic, and problem solving skills. *Journal of College Science Teaching, 34*(4), 48–51.

Harwood, W. S.(2003). Course enhancement: A road map for devising active-learning and inquiry-based science courses. *International Journal of Developmental Biology, 47*(2–3), 213–221.

Healey, M. (2003). The scholarship of teaching: Issues around an evolving concept. *Journal on Excellence in College Teaching, 14*(2) 5–16.

Hertel, J. P., & Millis, B. J. (2002). *Using simulations to promote learning in higher education: An introduction.* Sterling, VA: Stylus.

Kreber, C. (2001). Learning experientially through case studies? A conceptual analysis. *Teaching in Higher Education, 6*(2), 217–228.

Knapper, C., & Cranton, P. (Eds.). (2001). *New directions for teaching and learning: No. 88. Fresh approaches to the evaluation of teaching.* San Francisco, CA: Jossey-Bass.

Marbach-Ad, G., & Sokolove, P. G. (2002). The use of e-mail and in-class writing to facilitate student-instructor interaction in large-enrollment traditional and active learning classes. *Journal of Science Education and Technology, 11*(2), 109–119.

Marrs, K. A., Blake, R. E., & Gavrin, A. D. (2003). Web-based warm up exercises in just-in-time teaching. *Journal of College Science Teaching, 33*(1), 42–47.

Mysliwiec, T. H., Shibley, I., Jr., & Dunbar, M. E. (2003/2004). Using newspapers to facilitate learning. *Journal of College Science Teaching, 33*(3), 24–28.

O'Sullivan, D. W., & Copper, C. L. (2003). Evaluating active learning. *Journal of College Science Teaching, 32*(7), 448–452.

Ouellett, M. L. (Ed.). (2005). *Teaching inclusively: Resources for course, department and institutional change in higher education.* Stillwater, OK: New Forums Press.

Ratcliff, J. L., Johnson, D. K., & Gaff, J. G. (2004). *New directions for higher education: No. 125. Changing general education.* San Francisco, CA: Jossey-Bass.

Riffell, S. K., & Sibley, D. H. (2003). Learning online. *Journal of College Science Teaching, 32*(6), 394–399.

Stanley, C. A., & Porter, M. E. (Eds.). (2002). *Engaging large classes: Strategies and techniques for college faculty.* Bolton, MA: Anker.

Weimer, M. (2002). *Learner-centered teaching: Five key changes to practice.* San Francisco, CA: Jossey-Bass.

Bibliography

Albom, M. (1997). *Tuesdays with Morrie: An old man, a young man, and life's greatest lesson.* New York, NY: Doubleday.

American Association for Higher Education. (1992). *9 principles of good practice for assessing student learning.* Washington, DC: author.

Andrade, H. G. (2005, Winter). Teaching with rubrics: The good, the bad, and the ugly. *College Teaching, 53,* 27–30.

Angelo, T. A., & Cross, K. P. (1993). *Classroom assessment techniques: A handbook for college teachers* (2nd ed.). San Francisco, CA: Jossey-Bass.

Arnold, C. (1992). Seasoning your own spaghetti sauce: An overview of methods and models. In C. McTighe Musil (Ed.), *Students at the center: Feminist assessment* (pp. 51–64). Washington, DC: Association of American Colleges and National Women's Studies Association.

Baldwin, T., & Blattner, N. (2003). Guarding against potential bias in student evaluations: What every faculty member needs to know. *College Teaching, 51*(1), 27–32.

Banta, T. W., Lund, J. P., Black, K. E., & Oblander, F. W. (1996). *Assessment in practice: Putting principles to work on college campuses.* San Francisco, CA: Jossey-Bass.

Belenky, M. F., Clinchy, B. M., Goldberger, N. R., & Tarule, J. M. (1997). *Women's ways of knowing: The development of self, voice and mind* (10th anniversary ed.). New York, NY: BasicBooks.

Biggs, J. (1999, May). Assessment: An integral part of the teaching system. *AAHE Bulletin, 59*, 10–12.

Bloom, B.S. (Ed.). (1956). *Taxonomy of educational objectives: The classification of educational goals. Handbook I: Cognitive domain.* White Plains, NY: Longman.

Bonwell, C. C., & Eison, J. A. (1991). *Active learning: Creating excitement in the classroom.* Washington, DC: George Washington University. (ASHE-ERIC Higher Education Report, No. 1)

Bowen, S. (2005, Winter). Engaged learning: Are we all on the same page? *Peer Review, 7*(2), 4–7.

Bransford, J. D., Brown, A. L., & Cocking, R. R. (Eds.). (2000). *How people learn: Brain, mind, experience, and school* (Expanded ed.). Washington, DC: National Academy Press.

Brookfield, S. D., & Preskill, S. (1999). *Discussion as a way of teaching: Tools and techniques for democratic classrooms.* San Francisco, CA: Jossey-Bass.

Chism, N. (1999). *Peer review of teaching: A sourcebook.* Bolton, MA: Anker.

Cottrell, S. A., & Jones, E. A. (2002). A snapshot of scholarship of teaching and learning initiatives: Using assessment results to improve student learning and development. *Assessment Update, 14*(3), 6–7.

Davies, M. A., & Wavering, M. (1999). Alternative assessment: New directions in teaching and learning. *Contemporary Education, 71*(1), 39–45.

Davis, B. G. (1993). *Tools for Teaching.* San Francisco, CA: Jossey-Bass.

Driscoll, A., & Wood, S. (2004, Fall). Creating learner-centered assessment: A faculty-driven process. *Peer Review, 7*(1), 12–15.

Fink, L. D. (1999). *Active learning.* Retrieved January 12, 2006, from the Honolulu Community College Faculty Development web site: http://honolulu.hawaii.edu/intranet/committees/FacDevCom/guidebk/teachtip/active.htm

Fink, L. D. (2003). *Creating significant learning experiences: An integrated approach to designing college courses.* San Francisco, CA: Jossey-Bass.

Flavell, J. H. (1976). Metacognitive aspects of problem solving. In L. Resnick (Ed.), *The nature of intelligence* (pp. 231–235). Hillsdale, NJ: Lawrence Erlbaum Associates.

Gardner, H. (1983). *Frames of mind: The theory of multiple intelligences.* New York, NY: BasicBooks.

Gavrin, A. (1996). *JiTT learning goals.* Retrieved December 23, 2005, from the Indiana University–Purdue University Indianapolis web site: http://webphysics.iupui.edu/jitt/goals.html

Graesser, A. C., Person, N. K., & Hu, X. (2002). Improving comprehension through discourse processing (pp. 33-44). In D. F. Halpern & M. D. Hakel (Eds.), *New directions for teaching and learning: No. 89. Applying the science of learning to university teaching and beyond.* San Francisco, CA: Jossey-Bass.

Hall, E. W., & Salmon, S. J. (2003). Chocolate chip cookies and rubrics: Helping students understand rubrics in inclusive settings. *TEACHING Exceptional Children, 35*(4), 8–11.

Halpern, D. F., & Hakel, M. D. (Eds.).(2002). *New directions for teaching and learning: No. 89. Applying the science of learning to university teaching and beyond.* San Francisco, CA: Jossey-Bass.

Harvard-Smithsonian Center for Astrophysics (Producer). (1987). *A private universe* [Motion picture]. (Available from Annenberg Media, P.O. Box 2345, S. Burlington, VT 05407-2345)

Herreid, C. F. (1997/1998). What makes a good case? *Journal of College Science Teaching, 27*(3), 163–165.

Huba, M. E., & Freed, J. E. (2000). *Learner-centered assessment on college campuses: Shifting the focus from teaching to learning.* Needham Heights, MA: Allyn and Bacon.

Hughes, J. (Producer/Writer/Director), & Jacobson, T. (Producer). (1986). *Ferris Bueller's day off* [Motion picture]. United States: Paramount Pictures.

Instructional Development Services. (2002). *Instruction at FSU: A guide to teaching and learning practices* (4th ed.). Tallahassee, FL: Florida State University.

Knight, P. (Ed.). (1995). *Assessment for learning in higher education.* London, England: Kogan Page.

Kuh, G. D. (2003, March/April). What we're learning about student engagement from NSSE: benchmarks for effective educational practices. *Change, 35*(2), 24–32.

Lakos, A., & Phipps, S. (2004, July). Creating a culture of assessment: A catalyst for organizational change. *Libraries and the Academy, 4*(3), 345–361.

Lee, V. S., Mentkowski, M., Drout, C. E., McGury, S., Hamilton, S. J., & Shapiro, D. (2003, May/June). The evolution and uses of a framework for placing student learning at the center of institutions of higher education. *Assessment Update, 15*(3), 1–2, 14.

Loacker, G., Cromwell, C., & O'Brien, K. (1986). Assessment in higher education: To serve the learner. In C. Adelman (Ed.), *Assessment in American higher education: Issues and contexts* (pp. 47–62). Washington, DC: U.S. Department of Education, Office of Educational Research and Improvement.

Macaulay, C., & Cree, V. E. (1999, June). Transfer of Learning: Concept and Process. *Social Work Education, 18*(2), 183–194.

Magennis, S., & Farrell, A. (2005). Teaching and learning activities: Expanding the repertoire to support student learning. In G. O'Neill, S. Moore, & B. McMullin (Eds.). *Emerging issues in the practice of university learning and teaching* (pp. 45–54). Dublin, Ireland: All Ireland Society for Higher Education.

Magruder, J., McManis, M. A., & Young, C. C. (1997, Winter). The right idea at the right time: Development of a transformational assessment culture. *New Directions for Higher Education, 1997*(100), 17–29.

Marchese, T. J. (1987). Third down, ten years to go. *AAHE Bulletin, 40*(4), 3–8.

McKeachie, W. J. (1986). *Teaching tips: A guidebook for the beginning college teacher* (8th ed.). Lexington, MA: Heath.

Michaelson, L. K., Knight, A. B., & Fink, L. D. (Eds.). (2002). *Team-based learning: A transformative use of small groups in college teaching.* Westport, CT: Praeger.

Miller, M. P. (1996). Introducing art history through problem-based learning. *About Teaching #50.* Retrieved January 6, 2006, from the University of Delaware, Problem-Based Learning web site: http://www.udel.edu/pbl/cte/spr96-arth.html

Musil, C. M. (1992). *Students at the center: Feminist assessment.* Washington, DC: Association of American Colleges & Universities.

Novak, G. M., & Patterson, E. T. (1998, May). *Just in Time Teaching: Active pedagogy with WWW.* Paper presented at the meeting of the International Associations of Science and Technology for Development, Cancun, Mexico.

Paulson, L. F., Paulson, P. R., & Meyer, C. A. (1991). What makes a portfolio a portfolio? *Educational Leadership, 48*(5), 60–63.

Piaget, J. (1950). *The psychology of intelligence.* New York, NY: Routledge.

Race P. (1995). What has assessment done for us—and to us? In P. Knight (Ed.). *Assessment for learning in higher education* (pp. 61–74). London, England: Kogan Page.

Revak, M. A., & Scheffel, D. L. (2001, April). *A top ten list of assessment tools for academic courses and programs.* Paper presented at the annual meeting of the North Central Association, Chicago, IL.

Rowe, M. B. (1972). *Wait time and rewards as instructional variables, their influence in language, logic, and fate control*. Paper presented at the National Association for Research in Science Teaching, Chicago, IL. ED 061 103.

Ruhl, K. L., Hughes, C. A., & Schloss, P. J. (1987). Using the pause procedure to enhance lecture recall. *Teacher Education and Special Education, 10*(1), 14–18.

Schroeder, C. C., & Kuh, G. D. (2003). How are we doing at engaging students? Charles Schroeder talks to George Kuh. *About Campus, 8*, 9–16.

Singley, M. K., & Anderson, J. R. (1989). *The transfer of cognitive skill*. Cambridge, MA: Harvard University Press.

Svinicki, M. (1993). What they don't know can hurt them: The role of prior knowledge in learning. *Teaching Excellence, 4*, 5. Focus on Faculty. Provo, UT: Brigham Young University.

Terenzini, P. T., & Pascarella, E.T. (1994, January/ February). Living with myths: Undergraduate education in America. *Change, 26*(1), 28–30.

Wehlburg, C. (2001). *Program assessment toolkit*. Sarasota, FL: American Accounting Association.

Wehlburg, C. M. (2005). Using data to enhance college teaching: Course and departmental assessment results as a faculty development tool. In S. Chadwick-Blossey & D. R. Robertson (Eds.), *To improve the academy: Vol. 23. Resources for faculty, instructional, and organizational development* (pp. 165–172). Bolton, MA: Anker.

Weimer, M. (1990). *Improving college teaching: Strategies for developing instructional effectiveness.* San Francisco, CA: Jossey-Bass.

Wiggins, G. (1989). A true test: Toward more authentic and equitable assessment. *Phi Delta Kappan, 70*(9), 703–713.

Wolff, R. A., & Harris, O. D. (1994). Using assessment to develop a culture of evidence. In D. F. Halpern & Associates (Eds.). *Changing college classrooms: New teaching and learning strategies for an increasingly complex world* (pp. 271–305). San Francisco, CA: Jossey-Bass.